LAND
OF THE GOLDEN
CITIES

**AUSTRALIA'S
EXCEPTIONAL PROSPERITY & THE CULTURE
THAT MADE IT**

JOHN CARROLL

Published in 2017 by Connor Court Publishing Pty Ltd

Copyright © John Carroll

All rights reserved. No part of this book may be reproduced or transmitted in any form or by any means, electronic or mechanical, including photocopying, recording or by any information storage and retrieval system, without prior permission in writing from the publisher.

Connor Court Publishing Pty Ltd
PO Box 7257
Redland Bay QLD 4165, Australia
sales@connorcourt.com
www.connorcourt.com
Phone 0497-900-685

ISBN: 978-1-925501-59-9

Front Cover Design: Ian James

Printed in Australia

CONTENTS

Prologue		5
1	An Extraordinary Economy	11
2	The Australian City: Melbourne Case-Study	25
3	The Australian City: Sydney Snapshot	69
4	Civic Culture	81
5	The Nation's Myth	107
6	Nature	133
7	Threats	149
8	Conclusion	169
Acknowledgements		178
Bibliography		179
Notes		183
Index		191

PROLOGUE

The Australian Dream is there around the tables in the cafés in newly cosmopolitan inner cities, where young professionals meet to transact business, or catch-up; and others work alone on their laptops—in this, the local adaptation of European boulevard ambience and conviviality. It is there in the family home, that warm and cheerful castle crafted to the couple's own needs and taste, the place in which children grow up, where they play, the haven to which, even in teen years, they retreat from the big impersonal public world. The dream is there on the beach, under brilliant blue skies, the denizens sun-drenched, lazing in the warm golden sand; and others finding the cleansing exhilaration of plunging into crystal turquoise waters capped in pure white spume, bodies piercing the crashing surf.

Above all, the heart of the dream is to be found today in the cities, where nine-tenths of the people live. Clive James recently reflected on his first volume of autobiography, *Unreliable Memoirs*, that it was a happy book because it was about Australia.[1]

Most who now live in Australia view their homeland as a kind of paradise. At least they do so on the material plane. The Australian dream, equivalent to the much promoted, and challenged, American Dream, is less clearly articulated, but no less potent. And it is not darkened today—as in the American case—by the sense of it being increasingly remote. More at hand, it belongs in the here and now. Comfort, and a pleasant, easy working and living, are part of our dream. Contemporary Australian cities are marvellous places in which to spend a life.

It is a timely moment to stand back to reflect on Australia. The prompt is the long quarter-century boom that started around 1990, two centuries on from European settlement. This boom is a singular and extraordinary world achievement, one that tends to be undervalued here, and is often totally neglected. It has made the country the second richest in the world after Switzerland, as measured in mean wealth per adult. By the middle of 2017, Australia had achieved the longest period of economic growth ever recorded anywhere in the world.

Wealth is a cold and narrow indicator of anything much about a people, apart from their material privilege and comfort. Yes, that is true, but a prospering economy in an era in which the rest of the developed world has faltered, and even stagnated, does pose the question of what has made it happen. Was it a fluke; was it the result of long-term prudence and practical intelligence; or a slice of both, and perhaps much else? What kind of people achieved this? What manner of society have they created in the antipodes that has proved so well adapted to modern economic challenges? 'Antipodes' seems an increasingly archaic term. And they have done it in just over two centuries, a comparatively short period in nation-building terms.

This book, to focus its reflections, selects a particular lens— directed on the long boom and its causes. How did the land of the golden fleece become the land of golden cities? Wool was the basis of Australian wealth from soon after European settlement until well into the twentieth century. The country, as the saying put it, lived off the sheep's back. Since the Second World War, the nation's prosperity has increasingly been generated by the cities. They have become the centres of innovation and dynamism.

To call the cities 'golden', while obviously a metaphor, is manifest in a fact that is as puzzling as it is striking. It demands explanation. The quarter-century running from roughly 1990 to 2014 witnessed a quite extraordinary and unprecedented economic performance by Australia. This performance was the exception—that is unique—among the developed rich countries with medium to large-size economies. Australia's now has the twelfth largest economy in the world.[2]

The quarter-century boom is almost certainly over. As has been the norm in Australian history, the local economy is governed by international factors beyond its control—currently poorer terms of trade, a slowdown in China, wobbliness in the United States, and stagnation in Europe. That the long boom is at an end does not tell against using it as a device to probe the nature of the society that made it, as this book will do. Better understanding the society should help in planning how to adapt to more challenging times ahead. Moreover, in immediate post-boom years, modest growth of 2-3% per annum, and a stable unemployment rate around 5.5%, in itself reflect a robust economy, given the lean international context. The boom might be said to continue, if in a more subdued key.

The success manifest in the long boom has been attributed to major structural reforms to the economy and to labour markets carried out by governments between 1983 and 2003—as, for instance, stressed in a special report on Australia published by the *Economist* in 2011.[3] That report was titled 'The next Golden state?' George Megalogenis made the same case in a 2015 television documentary series, *Making Australia Great: Inside Our Longest Boom*. The bonus of a long mining boom and favourable terms of trade are also cited. However, these economic factors do not, taken on their own, provide a convincing explanation. They are necessary, but not sufficient conditions. Equally at play is a cultural factor.

Land of the Golden Cities

An economy operates within a social, political, and above all cultural context—one that is either constraining and inhibiting, or facilitating and enabling. The culture question concerns issues such as civic aptitude and competence; institutional modes; character dispositions; styles of energy, confidence, and morale; and the larger factors of identity, political legitimacy, and security of being.

The necessity for locating the cultural factor in explaining major economic transformation was established by Max Weber in the case of the English Industrial Revolution—the revolution that made possible the modern world. In his seminal work on *The Protestant Ethic and the Spirit of Capitalism*, Weber showed the inadequacy of material theories of why industrialization kicked off in England in the eighteenth century. Those theories were limited to economic factors such as trade, mining, steel production, and the need for sophisticated banking; to technological developments like the invention of the steam engine; and to political factors such as the British crown waging a series of successful wars against France, and expanding its empire.

Weber did not deny that such factors were important, just that they did not provide a complete explanation. He added the cultural factor of the Protestant ethic, which brought with it a transformation in attitudes to work and to saving, and a new capacity for systematic, self-disciplined concentration.[4] To put the nub of the issue: 90% of the population living in pre-modern Europe, say in Shakespearean London, would have been incapable of working in a factory or an office today, for they didn't have the self-control—qualities of self-discipline and a capacity for sustained concentration. In psychological disposition, they were more akin to the most tiresome class of fidgety, restless, impulsive, in short delinquent, teenage boys. So, modernisation depended on a major shift in individual character, a shift that depended, in turn, on a revolution in prevailing values and cultural orientation, one that included a transformation to child-rearing and schooling practices.[5]

In sum, an economy is as dependent on its housing society and culture as a light-switch is on the electricity that powers the light-globe. As if, to put it bluntly, offices, factories, and farms are shells that can function without the people who make them work!

This book marks an extension of themes in my own work, especially on the nature of Australia, published in essays and newspaper articles over three decades; in the edited book *Intruders in the Bush: The Australian Quest for Identity* (1982; revised edition 1992); and in an Alfred Deakin Federation Lecture delivered in 2001, titled 'The Blessed Country, Australian Dreaming 1901-2001'. The argument belongs within the wider context of my work, which has been developing a theory of culture, through five books: *The Wreck of Western Culture*; *Ego and Soul, the Modern West in Search of Meaning*; *The Western Dreaming*; *The Existential Jesus*; and *Greek Pilgrimage*. Some of the Deakin Lecture has been incorporated into this book.

The argument to be developed has a double focus: the cities and the culture. It is the city that has determined Australia's economic dynamism, and provides the key to the singularity of the performance since 1990. Australia is good at modern cities, spectacularly good. It has a talent for them that is rare—with the obvious contrasts being with the United States and Britain. For clarity, the two strands of the argument—the cities and the culture—are separated. Chapters 2 and 3 focus on the city. Then attention will switch to three chapters on the housing culture—its civic dimension, its grander myth, and the role nature has played in the national imagination, and in the spirit of the place.

Malcolm Turnbull has given the importance of cities timely and prominent recognition. On becoming Prime Minister, in September 2015, he set up a first ever ministry for cities and the built environment. Announcing his decision, he said:

> *Liveable, vibrant cities are absolutely critical to our prosperity. (They are) where the bulk of our economic growth can be found ... (and they are) economic assets. (M)aking sure that Australia is a wonderful place to live in, that our cities and indeed our regional centres are wonderful places to live, is an absolutely key priority of every level of government. Because the most valuable capital in the world today is not financial capital ... (it's) human capital.*

1

AN EXTRAORDINARY ECONOMY

The *Economist's* special report on Australia in 2011 led with the title 'The next Golden State', and was subtitled 'With a bit of self-belief, Australia could become a model nation'. Let me review the period of singular economic performance.

The cardinal facts are as follows. In the twenty-five years from 1985, Australia grew faster than all comparable OECD countries (the Organisation for Economic Co-operation and Development comprises the world's 34 leading economic nations). 100 units of GDP in 1985 became 225 units in 2010; compared with an OECD average of 180, with the U.S., the U.K., Canada, the Netherlands, and Norway all around the 180 level. GDP per head of population grew every year between 1991 and 2009—a boom indicator. Between 2002 and 2012 income growth was unprecedented in Australian history, with the possible exception of the Gold Rush.

Through the 25-year period both the top decile of households (the richest) and the bottom decile (the poorest) had higher income growth than in almost any other country. In the decade from 2001, the earnings of the top fifth of incomes went up by 32% in real terms; the bottom fifth by 26%; and the middle three-fifths by 27%.[6] There was no sign of a change in median income between the bottom 10% and the top 10% between 2001 and 2016; in fact, since 2001 income distribution has become marginally more equal. The real hourly minimum wage is the highest in the OECD, and is much closer to the average wage than in any comparable country.[7] In sum, among rich countries, inequality is distinctively low.

Economic buoyancy depends on a steady stream of new and expanding entrepreneurial activity, which in turn depends on investment. The key macro-indicator is investment as a share of GDP. In 2012, the figure was 28.4% in Australia, significantly higher than that holding through the rest of the developed world: with investment in the Euro area at 18.7%, the UK at 14.7%, and the USA at 16.2%.

In the four years to 2012, the Australian economy added 8% to its jobs total, a growth of one million in the labour force—an extraordinary figure given comparisons in the rest of the developed world, with the United States simultaneously losing 4% of its employment. This was not due to the mining boom, for mining accounts for only 10.7% of the economy (rising modestly from 10.3% over the preceding decade), and employing a trifling 2% of the total workforce. Mining does provide 60% of export income, and plays a significant role in contributing to tax revenues, and in enabling high levels of consumption of imported goods. BHP Billiton is the world's largest mining company.

The United States stands in stark comparison. The median real wage-rate in 2013 was no higher than that of forty years earlier. Linked, the country has gone from one of high social mobility, compared with stratified Europe, to one, within the OECD, of low mobility. It has become progressively more difficult for new generations of Americans to improve their economic condition and their social status. The once prosperous State of California has been bankrupt for more than a decade, and is now characterised by corroding infrastructure, run-down state institutions including universities, and a flight of innovative business. America, the lauded land of opportunity has turned into a land of largely unrewarded struggle and hardship, its national dream of making-it through hard work and ingenuity turned into a hollow, papier-maché fantasy. Ayn Rand's dark prophecies about the collapse of American industry, in her best-selling 1957 novel *Atlas Shrugged*, have been partly realised.

The proportion of Australian employment that is full-time is high, increasing from 80% in 2003 to 90% in 2008. This has dipped slightly since 2014. Earning inequality has been stable through the quarter-century from 1985. Employment growth was, in the five years to 2010, overwhelmingly in skilled areas—health care; construction; professional, scientific, and technical services; education and training; transport, postal, and warehousing.[8] In the decade from 2001 there was a dramatic drop of those living in poverty: the share of the population unable to provide adequate food, clothing, and shelter for themselves dropped from 12.8% to 5.7%.[9] There is little sign in Australia of the gloomy predictions of casualization and deskilling in the contemporary workforce, made by some leading international sociologists—in fact, just the opposite.[10]

Australia is the shining exception in an era in which many Western nations have been bedevilled by sovereign debt, unsustainable welfare budgets, and rickety banks. Government spending as a share of GDP is currently 34%—compared to 42% in the U.S., 49% in the U.K., 56% in France, and more in financially-crippled Greece. Through the first decade of the twenty-first century, annual Government debt ran at 10% of GDP or less, markedly lower than that of any comparable country—although this figure is now blowing out. And while tax rates are comparatively low, Australia has one of most progressive tax systems in the OECD.

Demography serves as a key indicator of national morale—

nations that lose the will to reproduce themselves commit a kind of collective suicide. Australian fertility rates have risen back to the 1985 level of 1.9 (average births per woman of child-bearing age). In combination with immigration, this produces a population growth of over 2% per annum. In comparison, some of the large European countries are on the edge of demographic suicide—the German birth-rate is 1.4, the Italian 1.3, and the Spanish 1.4. Demographers suggest that once the birth-rate falls beneath 1.4 it is impossible to recover without immigration, for the proportion of women of child-bearing age declines too quickly. The German population is contracting.

Concurrent with Australia's economic performance, life satisfaction has been strikingly high. Australians rate their overall satisfaction at 8 out of a possible 10, a figure that was constant between 2001 and 2008, and constant across region, income, family type, and gender.[11] Cross-national studies since the 1940s have consistently found Australians report high levels of wellbeing.[12]

I want to revisit here the possible sources of this sense of wellbeing in modern Australia, with a view to better understanding the surge of economic prosperity. The question broadens into the domain of national identity, and in particular the nature of attachment to place, feelings of belonging, and of being at home. Alternatively put, at issue is where Australians find their roots. This is difficult territory—charting a culture in the broad—territory through which one needs to move with tentativeness and caution, while testing provisional arguments. The high degree of difficulty explains why most economists have preferred to restrict themselves to one-dimensional economic explanations. Mind, the best economists do express humility on this front, as illustrated in two recent titles: *The Elusive Quest for Growth* and *The Mystery* of *Economic Growth*.¹³ And a rare minority have stressed the importance of cultural factors, from Joseph Schumpeter in his classic foundational works on twentieth-century capitalism to Michael Porter in his influential *The Competitive Advantage of Nations* (1990).

* * *

Let us first consider the economic argument. The wider context is a history of Australian prosperity beginning soon after European settlement in the late eighteenth century. Ian McLean has provided an overview in what will likely prove the definitive economic history of Australia for some time—his 2013 book, *Why Australia Prospered*.¹⁴ Since first settlement Australia has, in the main, been prosperous compared to other advanced economies. In the late nineteenth-century it shared with Argentina the accolade of being the richest nation of all in per capita terms. McLean singles out three boom periods: 1851-90, driven initially by the gold rushes; the post-war boom of 1945-73, shared by most advanced economies; and the recent boom that began around 1990.

The boom periods shared four characteristics: high immigration, high levels of foreign investment, stability in domestic macro-economic conditions (the way governments steered the economy), and low rates of inflation and unemployment.¹⁵

McLean attributes economic success to wise policy response and the quality of institutions, in particular in relation to the abundance of resources and fluctuating international economic conditions. Australia has usually been good at seizing opportunities offered in the international economy. And it has been resilient to shocks, both positive (such as the discovery of gold) and negative (world wars and economic depressions). It has handled resource booms so as to make them beneficial to the wider economy. It has avoided the resource curse that can accompany, say, an oil bonanza producing wealth in a context of social stasis and institutional complacency.

Four examples will serve to illustrate the argument. Wool was the country's principal export from 1820 to 1950 (with the exception of gold in the 1850s and 1860s). The Australian wool industry was extraordinarily efficient. The general economy in the nineteenth century combined land abundance with labour and capital scarcity. Wool was low cost and high productivity, due to land being cheap and plentiful. The only capital input was the sheep themselves, and they needed minimal shepherding. The moderate climate meant that winter housing was unnecessary. The high value of wool in relation to its weight kept transport costs down. As an example of adaptability to international challenges, when the price of wool fell, the sheep were boiled down for fat or tallow, which was then exported. Refrigeration from the 1880s allowed diversification into the exporting of meat. At the same time, there was the further diversification into wheat, which would become the country's largest agricultural export (by 2011, wheat exports were slightly higher than beef, and double the value of wool).[16]

As a second example, the Victorian gold rushes produced a need for food that was largely satisfied by government intervening to break up large pastoral estates and to facilitate small-scale farming in the gold region. The economy was thereby broadened, providing employment, and reducing dependency on imports. An indirect long-term benefit was the establishment of a new agricultural industry. McLean credits the wider response to the gold rush as the greatest example in Australian history of adaptability to exogenous shock: it included open immigration and low barriers to hiring or firing labour, and low interference in establishing and operating businesses.[17]

Thirdly, the first half of the twentieth century saw the emergence of import-replacement manufacturing industry, which developed behind protective barriers (a main reason that the Second World War was economically beneficial to Australia, whereas the First had been punitively costly). In the second half of the twentieth-century, protection became too burdensome and the need to internationalise moved policy in a more high-growth, free-market direction. In this outward reorientation of the domestic economy, the protection of manufacturing was reduced from a peak of 35% in the 1970s to 5%.[18] Australia has had two very high growth periods in labour productivity relative to leading OECD countries: the 1960s and the 1990s.[19] The first reflects the success of the high protection, manufacturing years, and the competence of the Menzies Government; the latter reflects the success of the deregulation years, and the competence of the Hawke Government.

A fourth example, crucial to the well-being and prosperity of modern Australia, was the decision of the Chifley Labor Government in 1945 to encourage and sponsor large-scale immigration. The key figure was Immigration Minister Arthur Calwell.

Further, the weak period in Australian economic history, the long half-century from 1890 to 1940, marked by the shock of two depressions and two world wars, did not damage institutions, or reduce public confidence in them. While the strength and integrity of the social fabric was severely tested by protracted economic stagnation, there was negligible social unrest.

The recent boom is distinctly different from its two

predecessors. Neither of the predecessors was difficult to predict; nor surprising. The discovery of a natural resource—gold—on the scale of the 1850s and 1860s, combined with the surge in immigration that it attracted, should inevitably stimulate wealth. The fact that the wealth was well managed is a separate issue. The 1945-73 boom is equally unsurprising, given that its buoyancy was shared across the Western world, as the shackles of Depression and World War were cast off, international trade surged, full employment was achieved, and mass-production was reoriented from war materials to consumer goods.

The third Australian boom is quite different, in being singular among OECD countries—the exception. Furthermore, it has only been dependent, and in a minor way, in its latter phase, on a surge in the export of mineral resources. Treasury Secretary Ken Henry said in 2005:

> *If, at the start of the 1990s we had predicted that our largest trading partner (Japan) would experience average growth of just one per cent and suffer four recessions over the coming decade, that a large part of emerging East Asia would experience a financial crisis and severe recession (1997 and 1998), that US bond markets would effectively grind to a halt for a period (late 1998), that US equity markets would experience the emergence and bursting of a major bubble (2000), that the US economy would experience a not insubstantial recession (2001), that significant acts of terror would occur in New York and elsewhere, that Asia would experience health scares like SARS and avian flu and that oil prices would rise sharply to levels not seen since 1985, most of us would have thought the next 15 years would be pretty miserable*

ones for Australia. Yet this has been a period of historic economic prosperity for us.[20]

The third boom, which is the subject matter of this book, is surprising.

* * *

Let me now turn to the cultural preconditions for the potentially model economy of the last quarter-century.

In the pre-modern world, land was the source of wealth, with agriculture underwriting the privilege and power of the European aristocracies. For that reason, wars were generally fought over land. Today, wealth is dependent on knowledge and inventiveness. The new empires are based on trade.

Since the Industrial Revolution, the city has progressively developed in size and significance, relentlessly drawing economic power into itself, and becoming the generator of new wealth. The dynamic metropolis is at the core of modernisation. Jane Jacobs concluded, after a life-time of working on cities, that great ones are the prime motors behind innovation, triggering multiplier effects.[21] Alexis de Tocqueville added a political slant, in his enduring classic *Democracy in America*, observing that democracies have, as part of their nature, a relentless centripetal drive, that is, an ever-compounding tendency to centralisation.

Australia is the fourth most urban country in the OECD—and this is in spite of its vast land-mass (not much smaller than that of either the United States or China). 90% of the population live in urban areas. Cities are where the people dwell, with greater Sydney and Melbourne accounting for nearly 50% of the total population of 24 million. Four-fifths of Australia's Gross Domestic Product is generated on a mere 0.2% of its land.[22]

That Australia is good at cities has become recognised internationally. The *Economist* magazine's 2016 survey ranking the world's most liveable cities placed Melbourne first (for the sixth year in a row), Adelaide fifth, Perth seventh, and Sydney eleventh. Canada also did well. *Monocle* magazine's list of '25 cities for living, working, late nights and fresh starts' ranks Melbourne second to Copenhagen in 2013; Sydney is ninth. Geoffrey Blainey has posited that Australia has two great historical achievements to its credit: agricultural productivity, which has fed millions of people throughout the rest of the world, and post-war multi-cultural immigration. Cities should be added to this list.

So what makes a city successful? The inner workings of economic and social dynamism are mysterious. One of the most imaginative of twentieth-century economists, John Maynard Keynes, tended to resort to metaphors—notably that economic buoyancy depends on 'animal spirits'.

Richard Florida, in his recent work on the 'creative class', has argued that location has replaced the corporation as the key economic and social organising unit of our time. In the last twenty years, the first question asked in meeting a stranger has changed from 'Where do you work?' to 'Where do you live?'[23] Business success is increasingly linked to place and to lifestyle—key people are drawn to where they want to live. In this context, 'most liveable city' becomes a primary indicator.

Recent literature from the United States suggests that innovative and expanding cities and regions (currently Texas, not California) are characterised by: low regulation and low tax; high immigration of people in their twenties from diverse cultural backgrounds, who are experimental and untraditional in outlook;

porous, fluid, and mobile institutions, with inter-cultural fusion, and links between disparate socio-economic groups; relatively high numbers in 'creative' industries (a better indicator than the proportion with tertiary education); fluidity between high and popular culture; strong research institutions; and openness to international influences.[24]

This is not just a recommendation for fluidity and mobility on their own. Peter Murphy suggests that Austin, Texas (which is doing notably well) benefits from being a liberal city within a state-wide conservative political culture.[25]

A concentration of creative and knowledge-intensive industries is increasingly important for economic dynamism. The creative class, according to Florida's taxonomy, centres on core industries, which include architecture and engineering; the life, physical, and social sciences; education and training; mathematics and Information Technology; and the broad spectrum of the arts, design, entertainment, sports, and media. It also includes the professions, notably management; business and finance; law; health-care; and high-end sales.[26] How many who work in these industries actually create and innovate remains a key but unanswerable question— likely a small percentage.

Peter Hall, in the most recent encyclopaedic book on cities, concludes that creative and innovative milieus need 'buzz', 'fizz', and a 'special kind of energy'—we are back with Keynesian metaphors of animal spirits.[27] Cities have a big advantage over towns because they allow for the concentration of knowledge and specialist services; and because their idiosyncratic and messy, dense, even irrational nature, is resistant to bureaucratic regulation. And it is resistant to over-planning. Their complexity and density produces friction, which itself can help raise the creative temperature. There is also a question of how *global* a city is, the argument that the New York's, London's, and Tokyo's gain special synergies because of their scale and concentration—this is an issue I shall address later.[28]

Dynamism will not do it on its own. To use a musical analogy, the power of Bach's Cantatas and Masses lives off wild bacchanalian energy, but this bubbling irrepressible force is contained within a tight structural order of immense intellectual rigour. It is the head-to-head wrestling engagement of the two complexes that produces the sublime power and serene beauty of the music. In just the same way, this book will argue, creative and innovative cities need a constraining and directing order to provide clarity, balance, rationality, discipline, and a capacity for systematic hard work. That order emerges from the domain of culture.

The issue critical to understanding what makes a successful city becomes what are the necessary and sufficient conditions to generate buzz, fizz, and that special kind of energy. The test is to map the sources of dynamism. Or, to find some method of taking the pulse of the city—as Balzac attempted in nineteenth-century Paris, by walking the streets at night, then pouring his impressions into his novels.

There is a challenge here that extends beyond Australia, to the rest of the world. The big question is what generates prosperity—a multi-dimensional question that involves economic, social, political, and above all cultural factors. At the centre of the mystery is the city. Yet, theories about what makes a dynamic, innovative, and creative city have not advanced, to date, much beyond the Keynesian metaphor of 'animal spirits', or derivative evocations like buzz, fizz, and excitement.[29] The major interpretative work remains to be written.

Oddly enough, this prosperous city question stands alone in

the whole field of social enquiry as the one of central significance remaining to be answered. The other big questions have already been addressed: questions of the nature of modernisation and capitalist industrialisation; the secularisation of society and attendant crises of meaning in a post-church society; the rationalisation of modern life; and the decline of community and social capital, and its consequences for social fragmentation and anomie. The work that remains in relation to those grand themes is that of minor extension and refinement. My subsidiary aim in this book is to contribute to the discussion about the mystery of prosperity, by looking in detail at one case, that of Australia; and within that case, two cities, Melbourne and Sydney.

Culture is the key to city vitality. Charles Landry sums up in his voluminous book *The Art of City-Making*:

> *My conclusion is that while industrial structure, business development, natural resources and location are vital, what is even more important is the culture of the place, its psychology and its history. This shapes the attitudes of its people and its sense of self, the story it tells itself and the myths about itself that it clings on to. This is the genetic code of the city.*[30]

Cities and culture work in symbiosis, each feeding the other.

2

THE AUSTRALIAN CITY: MELBOURNE CASE-STUDY

My focus here is on contemporary Australia. But the post-war period set the scene, because it was then that modern Australia as we know it today was formed. The preceding three decades had been seared by war and economic depression—in fact, the fifty years between 1890 and 1940 had been economically stagnant, with negligible growth in average incomes.

What followed the war was a long boom in prosperity, and an accompanying transformation to the way of life. Notable were large-scale multi-cultural immigration; the broadening of the economy including the development of a local manufacturing industry (heavy industry to complement the light industry that had emerged in the late nineteenth century); the expansion of home ownership to around 70% of families; the arrival of labour-saving white-goods and home appliances; new opportunities for leisure (with the granting of annual holidays); new mobility in increasingly affordable, and available, motor cars; and the pervasive influence of American popular culture, via Hollywood, magazines, and especially television after 1956.

The 1950s saw the establishment of suburban domesticity as the nation's predominant way of life.[31] It centred on building families and homes within a cheerful local community, served by shops and sporting clubs, with car travel at weekends and on annual paid holidays to the country and to the beach.[32] The car was vital to the development of the suburbs, above all providing access to a wide choice of jobs. In 1945, one-fifth of city trips were made by car; by the 1980s, the ratio had jumped to four-fifths.[33] With the further passing of time, the domination of the car has only strengthened. In 2011, across greater Melbourne, 65% of employed people travelled to work by car, 10% by train, 4% by tram or bus, 3% walked, and 1% bicycled (10% did not go to work on Census day).[34] The percentages are similar for the other Australian cities.

This new style of suburban living was qualitatively different to what had come before. In the case of Melbourne, the move to the suburbs had begun in the 1880s boom. At the start of that decade, 70% of the total population of 250,000 lived in the inner city, within walking distance of their workplaces. In the following ten years, the population doubled, with two-thirds of the immigrant population settling in suburbs, encouraged by new train and tram services.[35] The suburban ideal, centred on 'a home of your own', was born. By 1890, around 40% of Melbournians owned their own home, likely the highest percentage of any city in the world at the time.[36] It would take another 50 years for the population to redouble.

The quality of 1950s suburban life, and its ethos, has continued. It has been complemented in last quarter-century by the emergence of cosmopolitan inner cities.

Melbourne will serve as my major example, or case-study representative of the Australian city. I have chosen to treat it thoroughly, rather than spreading attention more thinly across a number of cases. The type of cultural interpretation I am employing depends on a *feel* for the city, and Melbourne happens to be the city I know best. The Melbourne case-study will be followed by a snapshot chapter on Sydney, Australia's one city with a claim to being 'global'. The argument could be applied with minor variations to most other Australian cities—expanding the exercise, and helping to further test it. Brisbane and Adelaide will receive some mention in later chapters.

Melbourne has been transformed from two decades or so ago, when it was threatened with the rust-bucket status that has befallen equivalent declining manufacturing cities in the United States (notably Detroit). The car industry was centred there, including hundreds of dependent component manufacturers, an industry that was steadily contracting, as protective tariffs were reduced. The State Bank of Victoria and a large building society had also just collapsed. Through the 1970s and 1980s, Melbourne had steadily lost its position as the Australian financial capital to Sydney—due, in part, to poor political leadership at both the State and Federal levels.

A quarter-century on from 1990, the city is a much more dynamic and diverse place, with a flourishing economy. Melbourne has ended Sydney's thirty-year run of faster population growth. In 2013, it possessed the four fastest growing postcodes in the country. As another indicator of economic vitality, in the four years from 2008, real house prices rose 31%, the highest rate in the nation (Sydney 6%, Brisbane 1%). The state has had the nation's healthiest government balance sheet. This has not been due to the national mining boom, for Victoria has no significant new mining ventures; rather it indicates fiscal prudence by State Governments from both sides of politics since 1992. A rise in the unemployment rate to near 6% in 2015, aggravated by a widespread loss of manufacturing jobs, was short-lived, and is unlikely to recur—given the precedent of fast recovery in the early 1990s from far more severe industry shutdowns.

In Melbourne's case, I shall argue that there are seven necessary and sufficient conditions for dynamism. Four of them characterize the city itself and they will be outlined in this chapter—a broad economy, high rates of multi-cultural immigration, topography, and a fusion of urban cosmopolitanism with suburban localism. The other three distinguish the wider Australian culture, and they will be developed in following chapters, under the headings of civic culture, the nation's myth, and nature. At issue will be the way synergies form, providing a case-study, and a logic which may be extended to other cities, in the general if not in all particulars.

a) Broad Economy

Compared with other OECD countries, Australia rates as a comparatively low tax and low regulation economy. With the share of GDP going to governments at around 34%, new enterprise only suffers moderate inhibition from tax burden and bureaucratic interference.

The Melbourne economy is broad: its major contributors being large corporations, banking, finance, law, manufacturing, transport, fashion, food, health, education, tourism, arts, and sport. This breadth played a major role in insulating the city from the rapid decline of manufacturing, and especially the car industry, in the early 1990s.

The large corporations include the Head Offices of BHP Billiton, the world's largest mining company (2015 revenue, $69 billion); of two of the nation's four big banks, NAB ($76b market capitalisation) and ANZ ($79b capitalisation); of giant retailers Coles, Bunnings, Target, and Kmart ($46b revenue); of the nation's near-monopoly telecommunications giant, Telstra ($27b); of the two largest transport companies, Toll Holdings ($9b) and

Linfox ($3b); of the largest IT company, Computershare ($1.3b); and of the nation's largest biotechnology company, CSL ($8b). In the area of successful new industry, it is the Australian centre for the creation of video games. Half of Australian funds and superannuation assets are managed from Melbourne. It is home to the Australian Council of Trade Unions, and to the national offices of many of the major unions. The city is the nation's busiest for cargo and includes the largest container port.[37] Victoria exports more food than any other state in Australia.[38]

In manufacturing, there are a diverse range of industries, including food processing, paper products, the remnants of the car industry, some ship-building, and a plethora of niche industries from clothing to aircraft parts.

Peter Hall's work suggests that strong creative industries are the key to a dynamic contemporary city. Leon van Schaik argued, in a 2006 book *Design City Melbourne*, that the city had become what Graz and Barcelona had been in earlier decades, the world's leading centre, for the moment, in design.[39] The claim is contestable, but the very fact that it could be made by a distinguished Professor of Architecture is telling in itself (the case is strongest in the field of architecture).

Local architects who designed a grand diversity of public buildings and spaces set the scene. They were continuing a tradition set in the nineteenth century by a score of outstanding buildings, including Parliament House, the Old Treasury Building, the Royal Exhibition Building, St Patrick's Cathedral, St Peter's Eastern Hill, the Princess Theatre, Hotel Windsor, the Supreme Court, two banks, the State Library and its Reading Room, the City Baths, and the Block Arcade. Walter Burley Griffin's Newman College (1918) continued this tradition.

Notable among the new are the Southern Cross Railway Station with a roof that flows in waves of giant steel bubbles (2006), a combination of lace-work bridge and 'cheese-stick' coloured steel pylons adorning the airport freeway entrance into the city, the 88-storey Eureka Tower (2005), the Melbourne Museum (2000), the Australian Centre for Contemporary Art (2002), the rectangular AAMI Park stadium with geodesic-dome roofing (2010), the Melbourne Recital Centre (2009), ARM's redesigned Melbourne Central retail complex, the Emporium retail complex (2014), the new BHP Billiton headquarters at 171 Collins St (2013), The Peter MacCallum Cancer Centre (2016), and a series of extraordinary buildings at RMIT built on the city's main axis—Edmond and Corrigan's Building 8 (1994), ARM's Storey Hall (1995), and a pair of 2012 buildings: Lyons' Swanston Academic Building, with playful multi-coloured and faceted façade, complemented by Sean Godsell's austere Design Hub, with its own intriguing multiple inner spaces. The block development of the QV complex (2004-5), while less architecturally significant, had the virtue of projecting the city's own principles by incorporating lanes and arcades, porosity to the street, and blending retail, office and accommodation space. Outside Melbourne, there are beautiful creations like Gregory Burgess's Brambuk Cultural Centre in the Grampians and his Uluru Cultural Centre.

RMIT has played a key role in cultivating architectural excellence, and in a number of other design areas. Leon van Schaik has led since the late 1980s: establishing a teaching program within which three schools of competing architectural theory and practice were presented to students, generating a dynamic pedagogy; and in directing procurement policy which resulted in RMIT itself commissioning a number of outstanding buildings.[40]

The twenty-five years of economic resurgence have coincided with a transformation in the place of art. Melbourne has long demonstrated strength in art—in teaching, in selling, and in production. The development of the National Gallery of Victoria was complemented in many country towns, post-Gold Rush, by their own imposing art galleries. Production highpoints include the 1890s Heidelberg School, Nolan, Boyd and John Brack in the 1950s, followed later by Fred Williams, and by contemporaries Rick Amor, Peter Booth, and Philip Hunter, and photographer Bill Henson.

It is during this recent period that art has become a central presence in the life of the city. There are now 100 private art galleries concentrated in parts of the CBD and some inner-urban centres like Richmond. Here is one of the world's largest concentrations of art marketing, generating around 2,500 solo artist exhibitions a year, and another 2,500 group exhibitions. Fringe spaces in lanes and alleys complement formal exhibitions, as does the new phenomenon of pop-up shows (renting a space for the duration of the exhibition); most universities now have their own gallery, collection, art budget, exhibitions, and curatorial staff; and secondary schools are starting to follow suit. Four or five major art auction houses alternate sales between Sydney and Melbourne, further promoting art as a major industry. Negative developments include a drift in art education away from formal training in skills and traditional art history towards the abstract ephemera of cultural studies; and the emergence of an art-buying elite that is less knowledgeable than its predecessors, and more inclined to decorative work.

Melbourne houses 4,000 design consultancies, employing 75,000 people, and generating $5b per annum. The city is the historical base for design in Australia, including the home of the Design Institute of Australia. Examples of creative industry products that have been sourced in Melbourne before becoming successful internationally include Featherston chairs, the Black Box Flight Recorder, the Bionic ear, lithium used as a psychiatric drug, a score of snake and spider antivenoms, the first influenza drug (Zanamivir), latex surgery gloves, the Triton Workbench, Lonely Planet travel books, Aesop perfume and toiletry shops, Staysharp knives, and numerous video games.

Intellectual culture depends on books and magazines. In recent decades the most innovative Australian book publishing has been generated by medium-size trade independents—notably Text, Black Inc., and Scribe, all based in Melbourne. Of the large publishing houses Penguin is in Melbourne, while HarperCollins and Random House are based in Sydney, as is the trade arm of Macmillan. The nation's cultural and intellectual magazines are almost all housed in Melbourne, as is the very successful *The Monthly*.

The Australian Ballet, with its home in Melbourne, has provided the national example for all of the performing arts. It commissions new work; and it continues to put on the traditional repertoire. It stages 200 performances a year in cities, regions, and internationally. It trains its own dancers, and maintains regional training hubs. It has achieved high ranking among world dance companies, especially during the period 1983-1996 when Maina Gielgud was Artistic Director. In 2005, it won the UK Critics' Circle award for Best Foreign Dance Company. It regularly exports talented dancers to the best companies around the world.

The Victorian Opera developed into a first-rank young company, under the founding musical directorship of Richard Gill—its 2009 production of *Don Giovanni* could have stood comparison in any company. The Victorian College of the Arts has served as an elite training institution, providing world-quality education, notably in drama, dance (linked to the Australian

Ballet School), music (notably improvisation and contemporary music), and production—stage management, design, sound, and lighting. The Australian National Academy of Music, based in South Melbourne, offers the country's best training for classical instruments.

Television production has historically been divided between Sydney and Melbourne, but since 2010 has swung to the latter, with three of the four major production companies now based there. Five series of distinctive quality have been produced in the last decade: *Summer Heights High* (2007), *Underbelly* (2008), *The Slap* (2011), *The Time of Our Lives* (2013-14), and *Gallipoli* (2015).

Theatre has a long and strong tradition in Melbourne, fed by a plethora of amateur repertory companies based in the suburbs. Amateur dramatics has fed professional theatre headed by the Melbourne Theatre Company. In the 1970s, a new theatre emerged staging plays with Australian stories by young playwrights led by David Williamson and Jack Hibberd, giving voice to local manners and accents for the first time—Melbourne-based, in two fringe theatres, La Mama and The Pram Factory. The first production at the Pram Factory was *Marvellous Melbourne*.

The Melbourne International Comedy Festival, started in 1987 and held every April, is now the third largest of its type in the world, after Edinburgh and Montreal, and Australia's largest cultural event—it staged 480 shows in 2013. It draws comedians from around the world.

Melbourne has long held the reputation as Australia's great popular music city, although there have been ebbs and flows.[41] Mushroom Records dominated the recording industry for three decades after its foundation in 1972. The ABC weekly television show *Countdown*, hosted by Molly Meldrum, was the nation's most popular music show ever, running from 1974 to 1987. *Countdown* played the pivotal role in raising the confidence and quality of local music, giving it an international presence.[42] And, the live music scene, especially in pubs, has provided the training ground for many of the country's most successful performers. In 2010, it was reported to attract five million patrons and generate $500m of business.[43] However, the focus of live music is shifting from the pubs to events, like the annual Big Day Out rock festival.

In 1992, trading hours were deregulated in central Melbourne, and Sunday trading was permitted for the first time ever. At the same time, Council by-laws were changed to permit dining and drinking on sidewalks. An explosion in café culture followed, driving the transformation of urban life—with pavement cafés creating a new ambience. In the first phase, before 1990, there were a smattering of cafés, mainly in city-fringe Italian and Jewish milieus; in the second, a proliferation in the inner city, which then spread out into the suburbs; followed by a third phase, of connoisseur and specialty coffee houses—often giving patrons a complete design experience, from coffee packaging, machines and crockery, to tables, chairs, and decor. *Starbucks* never took hold in Melbourne. Melbourne University Vice-Chancellor, Glyn Davis, has required all new buildings to include a café on the ground level. A Fitzroy café, *Industry Beans*, topped its field in the 2014 British Restaurant and Bar Design Awards in London, beating entrants from 60 countries; and a Brunswick bar, *Howler*, won the award for Best Bar in the Pacific Region.

The vast proliferation of cafés was followed by a similar profusion of new restaurants and bars, enabled by a liberalising of licensing laws in 1988. This rapid change in the culture of socialising paved the way for the development of stylish bars in the last decade and a half.[44] A life-style revolution had occurred, with people choosing to catch-up, socially and for business, in cafés, restaurants, and bars, rather than in the earlier modes of shopping, office meetings, and entertaining at home. By 2010, central Melbourne was home to 1200 cafés, restaurants, and bistros; 63 bars, taverns, and pubs; and 56 nightclubs.

Creative industry is linked to sport—indeed, the Federal Government sometimes combines the two, in a Ministry for Arts and Sport. The popularity of sport in the modern world, led by the Olympic Games, draws heavily on the ancient Greek inheritance. The classical world was in thrall of *athletic religion.* Plato conceptualised the ideal as 'beautiful rhythm', with the implication that a kind of aesthetic sublime drew spectators to watch sporting excellence—then as now. And sporting feats inspired some of the greatest artistic works produced by the ancient Greeks, especially in sculpture and poetry. The Melbourne Cricket Ground today is surrounded by some of the finest public art in the nation, in the form of life-size sculptures of sporting greats—led by cricketer Dennis Lillee in full bowling stride.

Melbourne is the sporting capital of the nation. Only London comes close in the world in terms of the number of sporting organisations within the city boundaries.[45]

The Australian Football League, based in Melbourne, has significantly higher annual revenue than rugby league ($506m in 2015, compared to a total of $350m for the two rugby codes), in spite of 60% of the national population living in the rugby states of New South Wales and Queensland. Australian football is local, invented in Melbourne.

Any discussion of buzz and fizz needs to take account of communal enthusiasms. The case of Australian football stands out, displayed in intense public discussion on television, radio, and in the newspapers—in Melbourne alone for six months of the year, seven weekly chat shows on free-to-air television are devoted to football gossip and analysis. Talk-back radio maintains a high-temperature discussion between experts and fans, generating a hubbub of opinion on rules, umpires, coaching, character, performance, and great past moments and players. Most workplaces and many bars and sporting clubs in Melbourne organise tipping competitions. The intensity and pervasiveness of the interest in football often bewilders newcomers.

The AFL has itself been innovative beyond its own narrow domain—for instance, providing ethnic minorities with a means of integration and upward social mobility, with access to celebrity status and high pay (the first African player, the first Muslim were celebrated, as is the special skill of the many indigenous players); pioneering improvements in race relations; and controlling alcohol to make games family-friendly. Half those attending Australian football matches are female, a statistic that makes it unique in football codes around the world. And, unlike soccer in most countries, rival fans happily sit in the same area, and join the same food and beer queues—chatting, chiacking, and commiserating with one another.

The large number and range of sporting events, spaced through the year, serves to build a critical mass of sporting buzz. They are spearheaded by the AFL Grand Final, held on the last Saturday every September, which usually tops the national annual TV ratings in spite of being played in the afternoon. For those who attend the game itself, the spectacle is unforgettable—especially when experienced for the first time.

Let me rhapsodize. The fan, emerging after a long climb through a concrete jungle of dark staircases and low-ceilinged spaces, emerges into blinding light, high up, and a panorama opens, vast and radiant as if on the day of creation, with the lush green of the oval below, glistening and iridescent, uncannily perfect, too fine for mortal antics; the huge semi-circular sweep of stands in front; and the Southern sky above, itself famously grander and deeper than the Northern heavens. All is heightened, from the vibrant translucent colours, to the scale of the spaces— the playing arena is four times the size of a soccer pitch—and on to the epic forms.

The game starts with a siren. The central umpire holds the ball aloft, pauses, then sweeps his arms down. The ball bounces then goes flying eight metres straight up into the air—seemingly in slow motion, its up-spinning rise mercurial, rising aloft, unbelievably high, in an intimation of grace that announces the sport's aspiration. Then down it comes. The game is on. 100,000 fans let go, the wave of accumulating sound—a primitive warrior chant in its tuneful pandemonium rising to a crescendo of tumultuous uproar—rolling around the stadium, and out across the city.

At the first goal, fans rise as one from their seats, propelled aloft as by some surge of jet fuel erupting from the viscera, ignited, and they scream their affirmation, scream as if demon possessed, like a person they don't know has risen like a genie from within. Already hoarse with berserk emotion, and it is only five minutes into the game, they scream out their Yes of triumph, their Yes of magnificence, their Yes of right order. Hours of pent-up anxiety and suppressed fear are let loose, now flush with a torrent of adrenalin. This is the local mass-scale bacchanalia, and yet it is supremely civilised in its orderliness.

The Australian Tennis Open, staged at Melbourne Park each January, has retained its status as one of the four 'grand slam' events in the sport, and is better attended than the other three, at Wimbledon, Roland Garros, and Flushing Meadows (Tennis Australia, based in Melbourne, has an annual revenue of $186m).

A month-long Spring Racing Carnival climaxes with the Melbourne Cup, held on the first Tuesday in every November, the nation's preeminent horserace—'the race that stops a nation'. The Australian motor-racing Grand Prix is held every March at Albert Park, 4k from the CBD; and the Australian Motorcycle Grand Prix is held every October at Phillip Island, two-hours' drive from Melbourne. The Boxing Day Test at the Melbourne Cricket Ground is the biggest cricketing day in the nation's year (attendance 91,000 in 2013)—and Cricket Australia is based in Melbourne.

The accumulation of events provides a near-continuous cycle through the year of athletic religion. The sense that major sporting things are always happening spins off into injecting local culture with extra dynamism. It is common to hear of young professionals with a cosmopolitan leaning, who take jobs overseas, returning home because they miss the football. In fact, they miss the city, a city coloured with singular football hues.

The breadth and depth of the sport-industry cluster in Melbourne brings a competitive advantage. The best administrators and ancillary staff in the industry, and many of the athletes, are drawn there—to be located in the same place. Competition between sports stimulates innovation, and the quality of presentation, in turn raising the expectations of fans.

Tourism attracts 2 million international visitors a year, and 5 million domestic. It generates around $20b, and contributes 7% of employment. Melbourne is Australia's main conference centre. London magazine *Condé Nast Traveller* conducted a survey in 2014 that rated Melbourne as the world's friendliest city—'the capital of cool'. Sydney came fifth.

There are numerous higher education research and teaching institutions—eight universities, with Melbourne University regularly ranked in the top 50 in the world, and Monash in the top 100. The universities draw upon a secondary school system that includes a score of first-rank teaching bodies, most but not all of them privately owned. Education is a major export industry, with international students contributing in the order of $5b annually to the local economy—they are spread between universities, vocational institutions, and schools. Melbourne is one of the most successful cities in the world at attracting international students. Making up 20% of CBD residents, their highly visible presence in the evenings adds to the general sense of liveliness (students as a whole make up 40% of CBD residents). Melbourne University even ranked fifth in 2014 for interest taken by American students, as measured by Google searches, in overseas universities—behind London, Oxford, Cambridge, and Edinburgh (Sydney came seventh).[46]

The nation's leading scientific research organisation, the CSIRO, with 6400 staff, is headquartered in Melbourne. Linked, the main agency applying science and technology to defence capability, the DSTO, has most of its resources based there too. There has been particular distinction in bio-medical research—notably stem-cell research and cancer therapies. Much of it is directly or indirectly linked to Melbourne University, which has developed the Parkville Biomedical Research and Teaching Precinct. Notable among the research organisations based there are the Walter and Eliza Hall Institute (650 researchers); Florey Institute of Neuroscience and Mental Health (550 scientists); The Peter Doherty Institute for Infection and Immunity (700 researchers); the Bio21 Institute (600 researchers), the Victorian Comprehensive Cancer Centre (1300 researchers anticipated), the Royal Melbourne and Royal Children's Hospitals (2500 researchers), and the Melbourne Medical School (3000 researchers). Melbourne is also home to the Baker IDI Heart and Diabetes Institute. Half of the nation's top biotechnology companies are located in Melbourne.

Melbourne University has played an important role in the creative life of the city, since its very early foundation less than twenty years after first settlement. It has served as a major patron of the arts through housing the Melbourne Conservatorium of Music; backing the Melbourne Theatre Company, the nation's first state company; housing and subsidising the literary journal *Meanjin*; and housing the recently revitalised Melbourne University Press, the nation's oldest academic publishing house.

The American literature on innovative regions stresses the importance of openness to international influences. Since the 1960s, Australians have travelled overseas in rapidly increasing numbers. For those in their twenties it became a rite of passage to see the world, to spend months and even years in foreign countries, including working there. This stood as an initiation into adulthood, through which the self was subjected to the alien and unfamiliar, in part in order to learn from it. The main destinations were, in earlier years, located in Europe; followed by a gradual switch to South-East Asia.

When travellers returned home they brought with them new ideas and new customs. To give one example of the consequences: Australian cuisine was transformed from the 1970s onwards, with British stodge steadily banished from the cities: this happened mainly as a result of upper-middle-class youth importing European (later Asian) tastes and traditions that they had experienced while away. In the same period, a similar internationalising of cuisine was far less noticeable in Britain and the United States.

A broad and dynamic economy is dependent first and foremost on the continuous emergence of entrepreneurs—'movers and shakers' to develop and create small, medium, and large businesses. There are two essentials: on the one side, driven individuals, with energy, ambition, and imagination; on the other, an encouraging milieu. Melbourne has some history behind it, as home to Australia's two most successful business leaders, Rupert Murdoch (in his early years) and industrialist Essington Lewis (the man who built BHP as a mining and steel corporation, developed shipbuilding and aircraft production in the 1930s, and served as Director of Munitions during the Second World War)[47]. Further, post-war immigration has greatly deepened the entrepreneurial gene pool.

A new phenomenon in Australian cities is rocketing entrepreneurship among the under-35s. Partly prompted by the fact that house prices have quadrupled since 2000 (Sydney and Melbourne), while the cost of setting up a business has fallen dramatically, from $5m to $5000 in the same period, life-ambition has refocussed. The registration of business names jumped from 1.5m to 2.0m in the two years 2014-16, with new names registered at 300,000 a year. The number of 18 to 25-year-olds opening a business account jumped 60% in 2016 alone. Start-ups are booming, with an 800% increase in the four years to 2016.[48] So, an indirect benefit of steeply inflated house prices has been the stimulus of entrepreneurial drive and activity.

As cautionary comparison, Tasmania is the one state in Australia that is struggling badly in economic terms. Yet it has the soils and climate that could make it a prosperous agricultural centre based on intensive farming of diverse foodstuffs. But Tasmania seems to lack the entrepreneurs, partly due to a modern history of low multi-cultural immigration (only 4% of the population is non-Anglo); to an ageing population; and to low levels of education. It is mendicant, living off the rest of Australia—the Federal Government provides 60% of the State's revenue. It has suffered, above all, from weak civic leadership. To highlight the general point, it has been a maverick entrepreneur who has built Tasmania's most popular tourist attraction, the Museum of Old and New Art (MONA), opened in 2011; and another, the most financially successful destination in the State, the Barnbougle Dunes golf course, opened in 2005.

b) High Multi-Cultural Immigration

Seventy years of multicultural immigration has seen the Melbourne population expand from 1.2m in 1945 to 5m at the 2011 census (greater Melbourne statistical area). Most of this expansion has been due to immigration, not to local births. The 1950s saw many hundreds of thousands of new Italian and Greek migrants, followed in number by Germans, Dutch, Maltese, and inhabitants of the former Yugoslavia. The last decade has seen comparable numbers of Chinese and Indian new arrivals.

By 2011, the majority population remained Anglo or Celtic, but it was down to 55%—those with a specifically English background making up about 33% of the total population. Southern Europeans (principally Italian and Greek) made up 15%; northern Europeans (principally German and Dutch) another 10%. And Asians contributed a rapidly increasing 15%—half of that component Chinese, a quarter Indian, but also 80,000 Vietnamese, 50,000 Sri Lankans, and 45,000 Filipinos. 30% of the population was born overseas. Half of the immigrants to Australia in the 2000s were from Asia, with 70% of them having some kind of tertiary educational qualification.[49]

As an instructive instance, Melbourne is the third largest Greek city in the world, after Athens and Salonika, with around 200,000 people of Greek ancestry.[50] They have made a major contribution to their new society, with a striking number of successful Greek small and medium-size businesses especially in the building, fashion, and food sectors. Successful individuals include architect Nonda Katsalidis, writer Christos Tsiolkas, chef/restaurateur George Calombaris, soccer coach Ange Postecoglou, and politician Petro Giorgiou.

Greek entrepreneurs have flourished in Australia. But their counterparts are noticeable by their absence in Greece itself today. Three explanatory factors stand out. The major difference between Melbourne and Greece is the culture: the social mores and customs, the economic practices, and a political temper that encourages individual responsibility and independence versus welfare dependency and the grudging attitude that it is the State's responsibility to provide citizens with jobs and look after them, their families, and the towns and regions in which they live.

Secondly, people who emigrate are, in general, more energetic, ambitious, and perhaps imaginative, than those who stay at home—bringing with them extra dynamism to their new country. The notorious 'brain drain' that can accompany mass emigration may be less damaging to the home society than a possible 'dynamism drain'. Thirdly, People learn from negative experience: *that was how it was done in Greece, and we know it doesn't work*. This will likely be accompanied by appreciation for the better ways of the new culture, and with ideas of ways to further improve them.

Post-war Jewish immigration has also made a major contribution to the life of the city—for instance, in Viennese café culture in Acland Street, and in individual contributions to science, medicine, law, the arts, and to intellectual life in general. Successful Jewish businesses permeate the economy. Some of the larger ones have been singularly generous in their public patronage, establishing an American mode of philanthropy—led by the Myer family, the Pratts, and the Smorgons (complemented by that from two establishment Anglo families, the Murdochs and the Potters). There has been little equivalent in Sydney.

The American literature on innovative cities and regions stresses inter-cultural fusion. Melbourne has, like Sydney, managed over seven decades to assimilate several million people from a hundred different nationalities and ethnic backgrounds. Over 200 languages or dialects are spoken. No ghettoes have developed: the standard pattern being for the newly arrived to concentrate their settlement initially in one or two suburbs, then steadily disperse into the wider city as their economic situation improves, and their children marry out.[51]

One of the leading indicators of inter-cultural fusion is the rate of intermarriage. 2006 Census data show rapidly increasing rates amongst the different ethnicities of marrying out, generation by generation. For example, the rate increases for those of Greek, Lebanese, and Chinese ancestry from 10% in the first generation, to 30% or more in the second, to 60% or more by the third.[52]

Intercultural fusion is closely linked to cultural porosity. The main indicator of porosity is intergenerational social mobility, that is the degree to which the social and economic status of children, once they reach adulthood, diverges from that of their parents. The greater is the divergence in wage, education, and occupation the greater the mobility. In the OECD, Australia joins Canada and the Nordic countries in having high mobility, in contrast with France, southern Europe, the United Kingdom, and the United States.[53]

Inter-cultural fusion is, at its core, a cultural phenomenon—its domain that of a sense of belonging. This depends, in turn, on cultural cohesiveness. Becoming a part of the whole, or fitting in, comes with its own counter-dynamic—with the whole itself adapting, to incorporate the new in ways that change it. A culture is a living, hybrid organism, and the more hybrid the more dynamic.

A play *Wogs out of Work* became a hit at the Melbourne International Comedy Festival in 1987, and generated, in the following years, a series of spin-off comedies, and a television series, *Acropolis Now*. Local Greek-Australians took 'wog', a satirical term used against them, distinguishing those of ethnically Mediterranean background from Anglos, a term with tones ranging from the affectionate to the derisory, and developed it into a characterisation ambivalent with self-mockery and a confidence that was earthy, ebullient, and brashly crude. The wider culture took to the adaptation with enthusiasm, and even admiration.

Robert DiPierdomenico tells of his own assimilation into the local culture through football, of how a stigmatised outsider became a star player and local celebrity, known affectionately by the nickname 'Dipper'—a word-creation itself redolent with vernacular Aussie tones of inventiveness, familiarity, and impishness, the association with the Big Dipper, a terrifyingly fast train that used to operate at the local entertainment centre, Luna Park. Dipper recounts the story of how his mother became proud of him, not for winning the most prestigious medal in Australian football, as he did, or being part of Grand Final winning teams, as he was, but when he was named Italian Sportsman of the Year. As prize, he received a bedspread—one which his mother still uses on her bed.[54]

Andrew Demetriou, the past Chief Executive of the corporation that runs the most successful sporting body in the country, the AFL, is of Greek background. He is a graduate of La Trobe University, Melbourne's third university, which has since the 1970s helped facilitate cultural porosity—as a tertiary institution providing many of the brightest and most able from recently arrived migrant groups with the opportunity for upward social mobility. Some of the university's best students in recent times have come from Muslim backgrounds.

The final of the World Cup for One Day International cricket was played in Melbourne in March 2015. A crowd of over 93,000 was in attendance at the MCG, a record for a World Cup game ever. It was a richly and colourfully multi-cultural gathering, happy and abuzz with excitement. 10,000 to 20,000 Aussie Indians were in the mix—mainly in the hope that India would be playing, which it wasn't, having been defeated by Australia in a semi-final three days earlier, a disappointment that did not seem to dull their spirits, whichever side they backed, many patriotic to their new home, some preferring whomever was the opposition (in fact New Zealand). It was a bright sunny Autumn day, the occasion spectacular, and showing off, without meaning to do so, the brilliant success of multi-cultural communion in Australia.

c) **Topography**

The aesthetics of a city and its use of topography, while hard to calibrate, are somehow vital to its temper. The Melbourne Central Business District is square and structured on an efficient rectilinear grid of streets that are alternating wide and narrow. Within the grid nestles an idiosyncratic rabbit warren of laneways, which give the city its buzz and fizz. Some lanes have turned into densely-crowded concentrations of eateries and alcove shops, accommodating a milling hubbub of excited conviviality. Also, the best restaurants, cafés, and bars tend to be in the lanes.

The symbiosis of avenue and lane is similar to that developed in Haussmann's nineteenth-century Paris, where much of the mediaeval city was cleared to make way for grand boulevards, while leaving pockets of densely-webbed locales, especially on the Left Bank. Peter Hall has linked this topographical revolution in Paris to the development of the city as the creative centre for philosophy, music, art, and literature.[55] This symbiosis echoes the tension between the forces of Apollonian clarity and balance and Dionysian tempest that Nietzsche posited as the vital dynamic core of any great culture.[56]

Melbourne's centre has been transformed in the last twenty-five years from an office wasteland into a throbbing heart in which fifty thousand people are now domiciled. In 2013 alone, the CBD population jumped by 23%. How has such a radical change come about? What are the factors that have combined to revitalise a dead centre, which had been surrounded by sprawling suburbs pivoting on local Shopping Malls—as caricatured in the English case in the dystopic J. G. Ballard novel, *Kingdom Come* (2004)?

The Director of City Design at the City of Melbourne, architect Rob Adams, has played the key role in overseeing this process over thirty years. In 1992, a city revitalisation plan was launched, titled Postcode 3000.[57] Above all, Adams was instrumental in reclaiming run-down or under-used office buildings and steering their redevelopment into apartments—hence enabling the residential revival of the CBD.[58] The very term Central Business District has been rendered obsolete, given the great diversity of activity that has developed in the city.

Civic leadership is critical to this part of the argument. Lord Mayors and city councillors with vision set the scene in the 1980s. Supported by State Governments, they backed Adams and others to steer the redirection of the metropolis. The Cain Labor Government initiated the development of the south bank of the river—Southbank—and drove the building of the national tennis centre. Then the Kennett Government (1992-99), whilst returning the State budget to balance, launched into massive infrastructure spending which included Federation Square, a new Melbourne Museum, a convention centre, a renovated National Gallery of Victoria; it backed the new Crown Casino, and directed the construction of a revolutionary new freeway and tunnel network.

Cities develop their own traditions, which bring with them styles of civic culture. Melbourne had a striking early history of visionary leadership. The first Governor, Charles La Trobe, insisted that the new town be surrounded by generous public gardens. Surveyor Robert Hoddle's 1837 foundation grid for the city would continue to serve brilliantly well into the twenty-first century (partly due to luck, as instanced in the lanes being originally intended merely to provide rear access to the buildings on the main streets). Redmond Barry—judge and politician—was a founding city father in the fullest sense, driving the foundation and building of the State Library, the Law Library, and a range of educational institutions including Melbourne University. He displayed prints of some of the world's great buildings on the walls of his office, signalling an ambition for Melbourne to build its own equivalents. One consequence was the scale of the major civic buildings of the Victorian period, which would have looked incongruously large at the time given the size of the town.[59] In the 1890s, the city, at huge expense given a time of economic depression, built a sewerage system, and a treatment plant at Werribee—Sydney took the cheap option of pumping raw sewerage out to sea, a decision that has bedevilled the city ever since.

Melbourne is a river city. It could easily have been a harbour city, with its centre fronting onto the vast Port Phillip Bay. But in a fateful founding decision its economic and administrative hub was placed upstream from the bay. A river city has a quite different ambience from a harbour city. Location along the banks of a river of modest width allows intimacies of proximity and fluidity, facilitated by multiple bridge connections. Specialist precincts can develop within easy access of each other, softened visually by the presence of water and tree-lined grass banks. Where the river is wide, as in Bangkok or London, and there is dense water traffic, the ambience is different. And in Perth, the river proximate to the city centre is more like a bay, and forms a topographical barrier too wide for intimacy and fluidity. Brisbane and especially Adelaide share Melbourne's river city potential. A river city is denied the spectacular water panoramas of harbour metropolises like Sydney or Stockholm.

The Melbourne river edge has been brought to life since 1990, and extended to the docks. Coherent sports and arts domains have developed, blending with river and gardens, through a mixture of brilliant urban landscape design (also overseen by Adams) and luck.

Federation Square, opened in 2002, has developed into the hub that the city never had. Locals and tourists flock there, making it always busy during waking hours, and often densely packed; people are drawn by the location, occasional events, busking, and major sporting contests projected on a giant television screen. Its topography is crucial to its success, set as it is on the north bank of the river next to the city's key bridge, opposite the main train station, and flanked by major tram lines. Its open space is undulating, rising significantly higher than street-level, and cobbled in red-orange and ochre to mimic the country's heart. The visitor gains, from its rear half, a panoramic view due west, over the top of Flinders Street Station. It is an expansive, dramatic view, taking in slices of the city in the middle to far-distance, bisected by the river winding downstream, and heightened by the grand infinitude of the western skies as backdrop.

Sport is housed eastwards up the river from Federation Square, linked by gardens and walkways. It encompasses the Melbourne Cricket Ground (football, cricket), Rod Laver Arena (tennis and concerts) and AAMI Park (soccer, rugby). Melbourne is the city with arguably the greatest physical concentration of sporting facilities in the world—including the Docklands Stadium at the other end of town. Sport Business International, based in London, has named Melbourne the 'Ultimate Sport City' three times.

Successive State Governments have planned and executed this concentration. The MCG over six months of the football season regularly hosts crowds of 70,000 or more spectators—possible because the city remains home to 10 of the 18 teams that play in the national competition, a fact that has no equivalent in sporting codes in Europe or America. The MCG attracts a similar number annually to the opening Boxing Day of a cricket Test—an event of special cultural force when it is an Ashes Test, against the main traditional foe, England.

Docklands Stadium, opened in 2000, itself illustrates planning vision. It was built as football's second venue to the MCG, and to replace Waverley Park, a new ground opened in 1970 in the suburbs at the demographic centre of Melbourne, on the mistaken assumption that sport is like shopping, and people will be drawn to what is close. Waverley Park was never popular. Docklands has flourished, becoming an essential part of the city fabric.

The arts domain stretches from Federation Square (Australian art, multi-media), directly across the river to the Arts Centre (opera, music, drama), the National Gallery of Victoria, the ABC radio and television studios, the Victorian College of the Arts, the Melbourne Theatre Company, the Melbourne Recital Centre, The Australian Ballet Centre, and on to the Malthouse Theatre and the Australian Centre for Contemporary Art.

There is some special significance to the conjunction of sport and the arts, and to their prominence in the life of the city. They stage public performances and engagements that add buzz and fizz. The classical Greek prototype had, at the centre of its cultural and religious life, festivals of sport and drama—from the annual Panathenaia in Athens, to the four-yearly Pythian Games held at Delphi.[60] In Melbourne's case, there are extrapolations, like the annual Christmas Eve *Carols by Candlelight* at the Myer Music Bowl, attended by tens of thousands of families picnicking on lawns, overlooking the city.

Down river, on the Western edge of the Melbourne CBD, is the new Docklands development. It is building critical mass for business and entertainment, housing the national headquarters for the National Australia Bank (NAB), the Australia and New Zealand Bank (ANZ), Myer, Medibank Private, the Bureau of Meteorology, the Australian Football League, National Foods, and Penguin Books. It remains unclear as to whether Docklands will develop cohesion and character—current impediments include mediocre architecture, a failed shopping area, and some incoherence of access.

By mid-2013, central Melbourne, including Docklands, had replaced central Sydney as holding the largest collection of jobs in the country—around half a million.[61]

The Crown Casino and Entertainment Complex, opened in 1997, played an important role at the time in increasing the pull of the CBD, providing a huge new venue on the south river bank to draw suburbanites into the city, and to attract overseas visitors. A drab and vacant river frontage was transformed into a dynamic hub with multiple attractions. It remains the largest casino complex in the Southern Hemisphere, gambling but one of its activities, complemented by nightclubs, dozens of restaurants, a cinema complex, Melbourne's largest ballroom, and three hotels, including Australia's largest. International tennis players and golfers tend to stay at Crown, as do a range of celebrities—

Tiger Woods was in residence at the time when scandal hit him in 2009. One reason the Australian Tennis Open is very popular amongst the world's best players is the combination of efficient organisation and facilities, the city, the weather, and staying at Crown.

Ten kilometres to the south-east is the world-renowned 'sandbelt' of golf courses, sharing with Edinburgh and New York the greatest concentration in one city of outstanding courses—in terms of quality of design. Preeminent is Royal Melbourne. Royal Melbourne's credentials rest less on its regular place in top ten world rankings than on the Tom Doak assessment in the 1996 book that has become the connoisseurs' golf course Bible—*The Confidential Guide to Golf Courses*. Royal Melbourne is one of twelve courses in the world that receives a 10 rating, and Doak writes: 'If I had to name just one course as being the best in the world, this might be the one.' It has hosted the President's Cup the twice it has been held in Australia—a biennial event in which a team of the best American golfers plays a team from the rest of the world, excluding Europe.[62]

Design ranks high in any list of creative industries, and golf course design merits a special place in any discussion of topography. It derives from a long tradition of European landscape design, in which nature is sculpted so as to harmoniously blend the wild with the cultivated—a tradition with high points in Renaissance Italy and the English eighteenth century.

The Melbourne CBD is surrounded by beautiful public gardens. The Royal Botanic Gardens reigns supreme, as aesthetic jewel. It is one of the world's finest examples of public garden design, set in hilly terrain rising from the river, adjacent to the Arts precinct. Laid out in the nineteenth century, it is characterised by scenic panoramas and sweeping lawns, hidden pathways and mysterious cuttings, rockeries, and picturesque shelters, all weaving down to an ornamental lake. Native Australian trees, from both temperate and sub-tropical regions, blend with exotic species from around the world. The careful placing of garden beds and planting of trees illustrates the neo-classical ideal of a beautiful nature in which the wild is integrated with the civilised.

The presence in public of outstanding design sets a standard, one that may serve to both lift the spirits, and inspire to emulation. A building like the Sydney Opera House achieves this exemplary status. As do art works, as they equally represent the greatest feats of creative imagination in the past of a culture, and its most insightful readings of the human condition. Melbourne's National Gallery of Victoria is one of the best medium-size galleries in the world in terms of the quality of its European collection. It includes what is arguably Tiepolo's finest painting, *Cleopatra's Banquet*—an art historian has gone so far as to judge it the greatest painting on canvas of the eighteenth century.[63] It also includes one of Poussin's dozen best, a fine Memling, two Rembrandts, the equal best collection of William Blake watercolours, and of Rembrandt etchings.[64] The Ian Potter Centre at Federation Square contains the best complete representation of Australian art housed anywhere. The Melbourne Museum, under the directorship of Patrick Greene since 2002, has built enthralling galleries for the display of its old and rich collections—including that collected by Baldwin Spencer (Honorary Museum Director from 1899), and co-author of what have arguably been the most influential books ever written in Australia, on Aboriginal life and customs in Central Australia (key resources for the work of sociologist Emile Durkheim, and for Sigmund Freud's *Totem and Taboo*).

In relation to liveability, climate too is important. Melbourne has a temperate climate, with mild winters—hardly ever lower than

12°C maximums and rare nights of frost; and with Mediterranean summers, with a handful of days of extreme heat, over 35°C—dry heat rather than humid, tropical heat. Within this moderation there is extreme volatility, with the weather at times changing two or three times a day. Placed geographically on a coastal rim, flanked by the vast Southern Ocean to the south, and the huge landmass of the continent to the north and west, Melbourne is a windy city. This helps keep its air relatively free from pollution. The climate makes possible botanical gardens that intermingle native flora— temperate and sub-tropical—with imported European trees and shrubs.

Over the same twenty years that the CBD has been revitalised, an inner city network of distinctive cosmopolitan locales—with buzz and fizz—has emerged. The London seed seems to have germinated. For example, Gertrude Street, Fitzroy displays innovative creative-industry characteristics, blending singular cafés and restaurants, elegant boutiques owned by local designers, specialist bookshops, and a diversity of eccentric shops. Fitzroy has become a concentrated centre for creative industry.

The website *Broadsheet Melbourne* (it has opened a Sydney offshoot) stylishly reviews what is on in the inner city in nightlife, entertainment, events, food, and fashion. It cultivates a three-dimensional ambience of food, city life, and living well—with which its main advertisers identify their products (companies that including Mercedes, Nissan, Schweppes, and the Bank of Melbourne).

An older body of opinion read Australian cities in a negative and disdainful way, stressing their spiritual deadness and cultural vacancy. Bilious members of the intelligentsia established a tradition that would run, virtually uncontested, for fifty years. D. H. Lawrence, in his novel *Kangaroo* (1923), opened, typifying

Australians, and especially the men, by a kind of blankness, a watchful evasiveness—possessing what he termed a 'withheld self'. Robin Boyd, Melbourne modernist architect and critic, focussed on the aesthetics of the Australian suburb in his book, *The Australian Ugliness* (1960)—deriding clumsy attempts to make houses beautiful by adding 'pretty' features. Donald Horne's hugely influential *The Lucky Country* (1964) caricatured Australians as lazy and casual, provincial and vulgar:

> *Australia is a lucky country run mainly by second-rate people who share its luck. It lives on other people's ideas, and, although its ordinary people are adaptable, most of its leaders (in all fields) so lack curiosity about events that surround them that they are often taken by surprise. A nation more concerned with styles of life than with achievement has managed to achieve what may be the most evenly prosperous society in the world. It has done this in a social climate largely inimical to originality and the desire for excellence (except in sport) and in which there is less and less acclamation of hard work. According to the rules Australia has not deserved its good fortune.*[65]

Finally, Ronald Conway's *The Great Australian Stupor* (1971) took a more psychological bent, returning to Lawrence's 'withheld self', portraying Australians as half-hearted sensualists with feeble ideals living in a 'milk-bar culture'.[66] As a part of this tradition, A. A. Phillips coined the term 'the cultural cringe', in a 1950 essay of that title: arguing that Australians were insecure about works of culture, viewing their own creations as inferior to those produced in Britain and Europe. Ironically, the very intelligentsia that denigrated anything vernacular quite often exemplified cultural cringing.

Signs of the dissipation of the whining cringe came with the comic genius of Barry Humphries. His principal characters, Edna Everage and Sir Les Patterson, drew upon the old image of Australians as narrow, crass, and vulgar. However, the portraits were ambivalent. Edna was satirised for her suburban housewife clichéd speech; at the same time, there was affection for her and where she lived, expressed in Humphries' live shows in his home-town Melbourne by his intimate knowledge of scores of suburbs, street by street. Les Patterson was a repulsive drunken lecher, who, at the same time, displayed such Dionysian vitality and linguistic flair that he served as an appealing contrast to the tepid intellectuals, the pretentious cultural sophisticates, and the snobbish English whom he mercilessly lampooned.

Yet, there was some basis to the negative typology. There were no Australian novels of world stature before Patrick White—indeed, White's *The Tree of Man* was welcomed by poet Vincent Buckley with excitement when it appeared in 1955, as the first great Australian novel. Mind, the story of Australian high culture had not been one of undiluted mediocrity—there had been, for instance, the stories of Barbara Baynton, some poems by A. D. Hope, and a distinguished art tradition from John Glover to Tom Roberts and Arthur Streeton, reinvigorated in the 1950s by the modernist work of Sidney Nolan and Arthur Boyd.

In parallel, post-war Australian city centres were drab, exemplified in grey buildings, grimy, charmless pubs and a narrow food culture. Stodgy, one-dimensional British food symbolised a narrowness of taste and lack of imagination. Still, the intelligentsia was blind to the virtues of suburban life, and with it the importance to a society of providing an environment conducive to family happiness; blind to the achievements in mining and farming, and in national development projects led in the 1950s by the Snowy Mountains Hydroelectric Scheme; and blind to the value of the cohesiveness and stability of the political culture that had developed since Federation in 1901.

Cities that are pleasant places in which to live play a role in shaping their inhabitants' emotional disposition and even their sense of identity. Australians travelling overseas in large and increasing numbers make their own comparisons, favouring their home cities—these comparisons are now driven by realism more than insecurity. (The popularity of overseas travel is, in itself, a sign of lack of insularity and xenophobia.) These impressions have been reinforced by changing international perceptions of Australia: a 2013 survey found Australia ranked as the most popular country in the world in which to live.[67]

In the 1960s, local cities still seemed provincial and gauche compared to, say, London, Paris, and Rome. Today, they are more prosperous, in the broad, than their European counterparts, and cosmopolitan in their own distinctive ways. Local coffee culture is now being exported, first to London and now to New York and Paris. A proliferation of Australian-styled and run cafés have opened in Manhattan, including Bluestone Lane with six outlets achieving the fastest business listing in the *New York Times*' Best Coffee Brand guide. Bluestone Lane deliberately recruits staff from Melbourne, ones bringing with them the local café DNA.[68]

Australian cities exhibit a new interest in food and dining, reflected in a proliferation of high-quality restaurants and cafés, much better produce available even in mass supermarket chains, and a splurge of television cooking shows led by the top-rating *Master Chef*—influencing a higher standard of home cooking. For the first time ever, Australians returning home from travel overseas, and especially in Europe, may claim with some plausibility that their country has the best food to be found anywhere in the Western world today. Yet, it is equally true that the nation's wellbeing is threatened by rising rates of obesity, due mainly to the consumption of junk food.

In the discussion of Melbourne's topography, I have surveyed the physical base, that of the land and its surrounds, and the way it has been developed by the settlers: a centre with its public buildings and cultivated open spaces, the suburbs with their houses, parks, and casual fluidity, and a transport network connecting the whole. Then there is the cultural topography of the city, the all-important way in which the ethos, the mental orientation, and the psychological attachments of the citizens blend with their habitat. Physical and cultural topographies interweave, each influencing the other. The cultural topography will be discussed at length in later chapters.

The significance of topography in reading the nature of a city was stressed in the case of Los Angeles by Reyner Banham, as long ago as 1971. Banham focused on what he called Los Angeles' four 'ecologies'—surfurbia, the foothills, the plains, and the freeways.[69] I shall turn to Melbourne suburbia in the next section.

d) Fusion of Urban Cosmopolitanism and Suburban Localism

One axis of the new Melbourne dynamism is the counterpoising of inner-urban dynamic cosmopolitanism with enthusiastic suburbanism, cross-fertilizing each other.

The new direction over two decades is illustrated by entertainment. The post-war trend was towards the suburbs, led by television in home living-rooms, drive-in cinemas, and cinema complexes in local shopping malls; complemented, as people reduced their dependency on home cooking, by fast food, take-away outlets, food halls in the larger malls, and local restaurants. Since 1990, the CBD and its urban fringe have built a critical mass of cafés, bars, restaurants, and cinema/theatre/sport attractions that acts centripetally on suburban dwellers, especially at weekends. The dead centre has turned into the throbbing heart.

In terms of liveability, the inner-urban is challenging the suburban, as reflected in the prices of houses and apartments. The appeal of living in the inner-city is even spreading to traditionally quintessential suburban occupants—the family with young children. For over a century Toorak, 5km distant from the city centre, was famously Melbourne's most expensive and exclusive suburb; CBD-rim East Melbourne has recently replaced it, as ranked by the highest median house prices.

The centripetal pull is also reflected in the number of sizeable businesses that had their Head Offices located in the suburbs twenty years ago, but which have now moved into the CBD or its surrounds. This holds for Penguin Books, Grollo Constructions/Grocon, Toll Holdings, Linfox, Foster's Brewing, and retailer Myer. Crown Casino played its own role, providing a centralised alternative to the gambling locations that had hitherto been suburban—attracting suburbanites into the city.

There were economic motives for much of this relocation. The Grattan Institute's 2013 Report on *Productive Cities* notes the case of engineering and consulting firm SKM. SKM moved from suburban Armadale, 7k from the centre, into the CBD, in spite of the new office being almost twice as expensive in rental terms, having no parking, and being set on a busy street. The business appeal of the CBD was greater ability to attract qualified staff, due to the central transport location; that clients preferred the easier access of the CBD; and the fact that employees readily bumped into professionals from allied high-knowledge industries. In general, productivity is much higher for businesses located in the inner city.[70]

At the same time, education remains predominantly suburban. People prefer schools to be close to where they live—as they do with most services, and above all with shopping. Furthermore, there are no schools of distinction in the CBD, and only four located in the inner-urban area, two of which are Government-owned. Most of the best schools are concentrated in suburbs 5-10 km from the city centre. Only one university is based in the CBD (RMIT), and only two others are inner-urban (Melbourne University and the Australian Catholic University). However, the magnetic pull of the inner city is beginning to change this, at the tertiary level, with central location becoming more attractive to prospective students—students illustrating the Florida 'creative class' maxim, that location rather than the corporation has become the key to where people want to be.

The Age newspaper published an Access Economics report (2011) on Melbourne's most liveable suburbs.[71] Striking was the degree to which people voiced attachment to their own suburb. Whether in Strathmore, St Kilda, or Scoresby they show the same local pride that was tenderly caricatured in the film *The Castle* (1998), in which the father builds such a strong atmosphere of belonging that the family loves its suburban home, oblivious to the fact that they live on lead-contaminated soil, under power pylons, next to an airport—with the house littered with the faux features that Robin Boyd detested. This is reminiscent of Raymond Chandler's loving topographical detail of Los Angeles, which his world-weary detective, Philip Marlowe, moves through, the city itself (actually its suburbs) transcending the ubiquitous human corruption and squalor that it houses.[72] In the late 1980s, RMIT students mapped the suburbs, finding quite distinct and different resonances across the city.

Linked, a high standard of municipal order and cleanliness reflects a kind of self-respect (anti-litter campaigns since the 1970s have helped make suburbs and country towns tidier). It also reflects a kind of communal cohesiveness and respect for authority—often lacking in Latin cities. And, as always, Australian cities are less harshly competitive and tough than their American counterparts.

Australian suburbs have always been good milieus for family life, and for the raising of children. They have provided generous spaces, in contrast with inner-urban density: ample backyards for children to play in, sheds to enable Do-It-Yourself tinkering, and gardens for pottering and modest horticultural creativity. DIY has become a way of life, supplied by megastores and encouraged by high-rating television shows. It reflects and encourages a spirit of self-sufficient, practical individualism—everybody can become an entrepreneur through renovating his or her own home.

On the other hand, a trend in new housing estates built since the 1990s towards large houses and small gardens may end up compromising the very values that have made suburban life attractive. (The size of new houses has started to trend downwards.) The suburbs are also threatened by increasing polarity in the value of property, between the high-priced inner city and the rest. In 1976, a third of suburbs were mid-priced; by 2009, this had dropped to a fifth.[73] Increasing inequality is compounded by the fact that, although only 10% of jobs are located in the CBD and its immediate surrounds, the most productive and well-paid ones are concentrated there.

Suburban life, in the narrow and the broad, has encouraged mobility. The casual, sprawling topography of the suburbs is amplified in the highly varied hinterland that surrounds Melbourne, from scores of readily accessible children-friendly beaches dotted lazily around the large bay on which the city is situated, to dozens of ocean surf-beaches an hour-or-so drive south from the CBD, to skiing in winter three hours to the north-east, bush-walking, mountain climbing, and trout fishing. Nature, in breathtakingly beautiful and manifold forms, is within easy reach—by car.

Mobility in the opposite direction has drawn suburbanites into the CBD and its surrounds. In part, they have been attracted by generously ample and porous public space, including gardens, playgrounds, squares and street-malls, walkways and cycling tracks along both sides of the river, and sports, arts, entertainment, and eating and drinking facilities. In contrast with Sydney, the people have developed the feeling that the city's public spaces belong to them, and accordingly they flock to them.

What is on display is a new form of neighbourliness and civility. It is not one based on neighbourhood, on people living in proximity to each other, which was at the heart of what made New York a great city, as Jane Jacobs saw it.[74] This new neighbourliness is based rather on shared interests, on people coming together from different parts of the city to participate in a collective passion—say football, or an arts festival, or *Carols by Candlelight*—and then going their separate ways at the end of the event. The experience engenders feelings of fraternity, belonging together, common understanding, and warm attachment to place. This neighbourliness may be looser and more casual than the traditional form, but it is no less intensely communal for that. It is helped by the characteristic local friendliness that overseas visitors notice and appreciate.

Suburbanism has been reinforced in the southern cities by a uniquely-coloured charge of communal feeling that coalesces around Australian football. Local leagues continue, but, at the elite level, grounds have disappeared, in parallel with the rise of urban cosmopolitanism (with one exception, and that is in the satellite town of Geelong). Matches are now played in the inner city. Fans commute in from the suburbs to partake of the urban sporting buzz, complemented at night by the fantasia of city lights and general hustle and bustle. The Melbourne enthusiasm for sport is highlighted in the fact that when major games of the alien football code, rugby, are staged, they can attract crowds of 90,000—half of those present likely don't know the rules.

Jonathan Mills, as Artistic Director of the Melbourne Festival in 2000-2001, staged cultural events that attracted suburbanites into the city centre as never before. Bach 2000 concerts brought the world's finest Bach groups to Melbourne, and used churches, theatres, and concert halls to present the breadth of the work over two weeks. The Festival climaxed with the Collegium Vocale Ghent and the Bach Collegium Japan joining in unique collaboration to present three-and-a-half hours of virtuoso *St Matthew Passion*.

The Alfred Deakin Federation Lectures in 2001 drew eminent international and local thinkers in both the humanities and the sciences to present 40 lectures at the Capitol Theatre and the Town Hall—tickets were mostly sold out in three days, and the venues drew capacity audiences of 600 and 1500.[75] Both festivals brought a fortnight of buzz to the city. This tradition was institutionalised with the opening of the Wheeler Centre in 2010, located behind the State Library, a centre that curates and hosts a stream of daily, free public talks throughout the year.

On the urban side, there is recognition that the nation has become highly competent at running major international events such as the Australian Tennis Open, the Motor Grand Prix, the President's Cup, and the 2000 Sydney Olympics—which received superlative accolades in the British and French press. Such events stand as hallmark illustrations of the nation's capacity for large-scale organisation.[76]

It is quite likely in the coming decades that momentum will swing back towards the suburbs as the middle to inner cities become too expensive for young families to buy into, and commuting delays by either car or public transport become too painful. Joel Kotkin has suggested that 'aspirational cities' will be key economic drivers of the future, as they already are, in part, in the United States—cities like Houston and Phoenix.[77] Australian suburbs are ideally placed to develop new business hubs.

* * *

Conclusions

I am suggesting that the contemporary city holds the key to the big question of economic prosperity in Australia. It is the key to the essential cultural factors driving, guiding, and furthering prosperity. What may we conclude from the Melbourne case-study? To introduce another metaphor: there are necessary chemical elements and there is a crucible. The question then narrows down to which elements have combined together to make combustion?

Models taken from other cities do not seem fruitful. Melbourne has topographical similarities to nineteenth-century Paris, but the socio-economic conditions are very different, and Paris's centre had no periphery—what they do have in common is a strong café culture. Los Angeles' vitality centres in distinctive suburbs, separate from an inconsequential centre. Melbourne is more like London in being composed of a patchwork of communities surrounding the centre, each with their own distinctive character. It also shares with London a diversity and complexity that defies over-planning, or too much tidying up. Peter Rees, London's City Planning Officer, has argued that a complete city is a dead city: Paris is too 'fixed, composed, precious' to have been free enough to become a world financial centre[78] (a limitation shared with the French language—its classical rigidity of grammar and vocabulary contrasting with the fluidity of English, and its receptivity to new words and expressions). London differs from Melbourne in having no single central hub drawing people centripetally from its vast surrounds. But it is much larger.

Two decades ago the argument was put that global cities are a species unto themselves, with unique strengths.[79] London, New York, and Tokyo, because of their large concentrations of finance and its allied institutions, have scale advantages over smaller cities that spill out beneficially across life, business, and culture. The persuasiveness of this thesis remains unclear—Tokyo's subsequent decline might be taken as a counter. Mega-cities like Mexico City and Manila show that size on its own does not work. Also, there is no clear specification of the size at which a city enters the 'global' category.

Liveability is not an absolutely necessary condition for dynamism. London is unlikely to ever do well in liveability rankings, but it remains both an economic powerhouse and a creative centre—in part, because of its 'global city' characteristics.

One school of thought holds that friction plays a key role in creative cities: the very mess, complexity, chaos, and turbulence to be found in a large, dense metropolis is generative of creative energy. Proximity and density not only facilitate contact and exchange, but the concentration of shoulder-to-shoulder living and working generates a collective hubbub of energy and action, in contrast with the sedate quietude of a country town.

Obversely, there is the issue of when discomfort becomes so great that mobile people start to move away. California exemplifies: with America's highest State taxation and fourth highest level of unemployment, it has driven many large companies like Toyota to move their headquarters away, often to Texas, which is now the country's largest exporter of hi-tech goods.

Discomfort would include punitively expensive housing; clogged roads and inadequate public transport; high taxes and regulation; and a declining educational system. A period of rapid growth, such as being experienced by Melbourne, is at risk of tipping into its opposite, if urban infrastructure fails to keep up—an issue of civic leadership.

Whatever the size of the city, and the levels of friction, critical mass remains the key to the argument. Critical mass depends on the steady emergence of entrepreneurs, from the boutique shopkeeper through the building contractor to the corporation executive—new green shoots bursting out of fertile undergrowth as old plants wither and die. It depends on concentrations of creative and innovative people and their businesses, people with drive, imagination, and perseverance. It depends on buoyant morale, intense competition, and a striving for excellence. And it depends on strong identification with place, its look and feel, and its ways.

In Melbourne's case, we may conclude from the argument that has been put that other factors have been necessary to generate a broad economy, to attract and manage high multi-cultural immigration, to capitalise on the topography, and to develop urban-suburban cross-fertilization. There are six such factors. They contribute to the critical mass.

Firstly, there is leadership: people with the planning vision able to exploit the city's topographical potential and economic strengths. City leaders prepare the soil in which entrepreneurial seeds may grow—those leaders today are predominantly politicians and public servants, at both the State Government and City Council levels. In what is arguably the greatest Western paradigm—the golden age in classical Athens, which lasted for the half-century between 480 and 430 BC—the city was blessed with a series of four brilliant leaders (Themistokles, Kimon, Aristides, and Perikles). That era was followed by the rapid decline of the city, culminating in the loss of what should have been an unlosable thirty-year war against Sparta, which was economically the far weaker state. The Athenian case confirmed the old maxim that the fish starts stinking from the head.

Secondly, there is the presence of examples of excellence in architecture, design, research discovery, organisation, sporting performance, and the style of public venues like cafés, restaurants, and bars. Banham stressed the role examples of architectural excellence played in the quality of Los Angeles as a city.[80] Excellence is uplifting to the spirit, stimulating to the imagination, and a tonic to the creative juices. Mediocrity breeds mediocrity; dullness spawns dullness; and the mediocre appoint the mediocre. Melbourne's current growth spurt brings with it the risk of an incoherent proliferation of skyscrapers of low architectural merit. The even greater risk is of an emerging city skyline that has little to distinguish it from other recently booming cities around the world—given the internationalisation of skyscraper design. Rob Adams warns of Melbourne becoming Hong Kong without the views.

Thirdly, many exemplary secondary schools play a pivotal role in preparing confident and disciplined individuals. The way a society brings up its children sets the scene for the future.

Fourthly, a porous, tolerant society, and one that is economically buoyant, attracts migrants and offers them ready opportunities for improving their social and economic condition. The characteristics of that porous society will be elaborated in the next chapter, on Australian civic culture.

Fifthly, the growth of inner-urban bohemian buzz accompanied by design and life-style flair has injected a new dynamism into city life. It is as if the city has come alive for the first time since the booming nineteenth-century gold-rush era, which reached its zenith in the 'Marvellous Melbourne' of the 1880s. What had hitherto been embryonic has evolved; hidden and unimagined potential is in the process of being realised. Much of this defies planning, and reminds us that cities can over-plan, and over-planning is stifling.

And sixthly, a culture of movement prevails, from international and interstate travel, to mobility within the city, between suburbs, and to beaches and other recreation sites.

In 2013, London's Telegraph Travel, responding to Melbourne's third year in a row ranked as the world's most liveable city, wrote: 'Caffeine-fuelled, sports mad, and outward looking, Melbourne is unquestionably Australia's most exciting and diverse metropolis.' It has become the city that young people from other Australian cities, particularly Brisbane and Perth, and from New Zealand, migrate to—because it's seen as the cultural hub. Buoyant young people with confidence and energy inject buzz and fizz.

3

THE AUSTRALIAN CITY: SYDNEY SNAPSHOT

Sydney is, quite simply, spectacular. First and foremost, it is quintessential Australia, emblem of the nation's utopian look and experience: bright sun over glistening waters, whether harbour or ocean, surf beaches, and a balmy semi-tropical climate. Its qualities are visual and sensual. It is also Australia's one global city. This chapter takes a snapshot view of Sydney, charting its highlights without going into the detailed analysis provided in the Melbourne case-study. It is particularly concerned with differences, rather than with what the cities share in common, and share with other Australian cities.

An icon is a clear and distinct religious image charged with powerful sacred meaning, instantly recognisable and inducing reverence—highlighted during the European Middle Ages in glowing paintings of the Virgin. In the secular modern world, Sydney is the Australian icon. Bondi exemplifies. A 1929 poster commissioned to promote Bondi shows beach and surf in vivid Impressionist colours, being nonchalantly gazed down at from the Dressing Pavilion by three women clad in brilliant yellows, blues, and reds, as a handsome lifesaver approaches. *It is good to be alive here!* The cheerful optimism is infectious.

Bondi was the first surf lifesaving club in Australia, formed in 1907. It soon became famous in newsreel and magazine as emblem of the Australian lifestyle. Bronzed men and women lifesavers were projected as the human ideal—volunteers risking their lives to save those struggling to stay afloat in the surf. The picture was completed in surfing carnivals with boats competing as they plunged through tempestuous breakers, teams marching on the beaches with their distinctive caps and flags, a military order suggestive of the Anzac tradition, with war displaced into sport—here the athletic challenge of taking on a powerful Nature, and taming it. Above all, a lithe muscular outdoor vitality was on show.

Sydney is memorably a city of landscape. The harbour leads. Tens of thousands of houses are blessed with harbour views, or glimpses, thanks to the many fingers of water and coves, and Sydney's hilly terrain. There is also some exemplary public design. One of the world's great pieces of landscape architecture is the sweep from the Opera House up from the harbour's edge at Farm Cove through the Botanical Gardens, on through the Domain housing the Art Gallery of New South Wales, to the walks of Hyde Park flanking the CBD, including the Apollo Fountain, and ending at the Anzac Memorial. Sydney boasts many engaging streetscapes, again enabled by hilly terrain, winding tree-canopied streets, and a subtropical climate—for instance, in Paddington and Glebe.

Circular Quay is the heart of the city, a throbbing sea terminus with ferries steaming in and out, flanked by the Bridge on one side, the Opera House on the other. The Quay provides the uniquely pleasing and strangely beguiling viewer experience of a teeming waterway, with many and varied boats, ferries, and ships going about their business. It opens onto its own finely proportioned harbour seascape, completed by the grinning fun Mouth of Luna Park on the northern shore opposite, to the left of the Bridge, and Taronga Park Zoo to the right.

The Manly Ferry is as salient to the iconography of Sydney as Bondi. The first-time experience is unforgettable: of travelling up the Harbour on this Ferry, followed by a short walk to the vista of another golden beach, framing a broad timeless expanse of ocean breakers rolling in from the vast Pacific Ocean. *Home & Away*, a soap opera which started in 1988 (the nation's second longest running), is filmed at Palm Beach, further north up this coast. It projects the same utopian image of bright blue skies, golden beach, azure blue ocean, and semi-tropical warmth—part of the reason for its success in the comparatively greyer and damper United Kingdom (where, Australian musician Nick Cave, who lives in London, quipped, the sun never shines).

Visitors to Sydney with local friends will typically be taken on a guided tour, proudly showing off the city—invariably featuring the Harbour. The feel of the place has some affinity with Catholicism and the earthy atmospherics of the Roman Church's interior spaces, from the visual splendour of marble, gilt, statues of saints, chapels crammed with lit candles, Gregorian chanting, all suffused with the fragrance of incense. Sydney has a notable Catholic tinge and past—home to the nation's one Cardinal, and with a Labor Party and culture that is strongly Irish. The 2011 Census recorded its population as 28% Catholic. In parallel, Anglicans were twice as numerous in nineteenth-century Sydney as the harder-core Protestant churches, whereas in Victoria, the Presbyterians, Methodists, and other nonconformists outnumbered the Anglicans.[81] A visual and tactile bias in Sydney culture, steeped in lush tropical fecundity and its sweet fragrances, contrasts with a more austere and intellectual, climatically cooler cast to Melbourne.

Sydney is the single Australian city that can lay claim to global status. Starting at the symbolic level, two human constructions provide a visual signature instantly recognisable around the world—Opera House and Harbour Bridge. The opening of the Opera House in 1973 provoked anxiety down south in Melbourne; where it was felt that having no equivalent building signalled inferiority—public discussion followed, and talks of a competition to design a singular monument, all of which led to nothing of moment. A Sydney joke was that the southern city should erect a tower with the number '2' on top.

The Harbour Bridge, opened in 1932, was one of the world's engineering marvels, with a 500 metre steel arch—the widest and almost longest bridge span at the time anywhere in the world. The completion of the Bridge brought immense national pride, which helped offset the gloom of the Great Depression.

The Sydney Opera House may lay plausible claim to being the greatest piece of public architecture built in the twentieth century. It exists because of the extraordinary civic foresight and leadership of State Premier Joseph Cahill, starting with the decision to appoint Finnish-American architect, Eero Saarinen, as the sole judge of entries. Danish architect Joern Utzon was selected in 1957, his sketchy plans chosen above 230 other designs. If a committee of architects had been left to choose the winner there is negligible chance that such a revolutionary design would have won—Sydney would have likely ended up with an undistinguished civic structure reflecting the taste of the time.

Whereas the Sydney CBD is a squeeze of graceless buildings, its dismal aesthetic is magnificently offset by Opera House and Harbour Bridge, and the grand panorama of the harbour itself.

From 1890, Sydney outpaced Melbourne in population growth, to become the nation's largest city, today roughly 10% larger than Melbourne, although the gap is closing. In 2017, it passed the 5 million mark.

It has benefited since 1945 from the same volume and diversity of multi-cultural immigration as Melbourne. However, the proportions differ. Those in the Census who claim English, Scottish, and Irish background add to 37% (23%, 6%, and 8% respectively). Chinese are 8% and Indian 3%. The Continental European figures are lower than Melbourne, with 4% Italian, 3% Greek, and 2% German. Also standing out is a significant Lebanese component at 4%, which has brought with it a specific Sydney crime and terrorism problem. A further 27% of Sydneysiders claim an Australian background—the overwhelming majority of them Anglo-Celtic in origin. We may conclude that today only just over half of the inhabitants of Sydney, as is the case in Melbourne, have a British or Irish background. This contrasts with Perth, Adelaide, and Hobart, which remain more typical of the old Australia, having overwhelmingly Anglo populations.

Sydney is the nation's finance centre, a position it took over from Melbourne in the 1970s and 80s. It is now home to the head offices of three-quarters of domestic and international banks, including the two largest local banks—CBA and Westpac. It is the centre for merchant banking, led by the Macquarie Bank, the largest investment house in the country ($2b profit in 2016), a bank boasting a plethora of international interests. The Reserve Bank of Australia has its head office in Sydney, and both the Australia Stock Exchange and the Futures Exchange are based there. The Australian Securities and Investments Commission is also headquartered in Sydney.

Whereas British companies in the nineteenth-century tended to locate their Australian branches in Melbourne, partly because Melbourne was the earlier port of call on the voyage from Britain, since 1945 international companies have, in the main, situated their Australian offices in Sydney—especially American and Japanese ones. Top executives choose where to locate their overseas branches: they can afford, with their own high incomes, houses and apartments with harbour views—so why wouldn't they choose Sydney?

Sydney is the country's undisputed tourism capital, a magnet to overseas visitors drawn by the very qualities I have been sketching. 300 cruise ships visit a year. Tourism generates over $30b per annum, care of 30 million plus visitors. In 2016 there were 3.8m overseas visitors (compared with 2.6m to Victoria, and 2.5m to Queensland). From the start of the age of the Jumbo jet, Sydney has been the main point of entry from overseas into Australia, with multiple times more daily international flights than any other airport. Kingsford Smith Airport, as the national air transport hub, has facilitated both tourism and business.

Information and Communications Technology is a mixed story, with the larger local companies and software innovation more concentrated in Melbourne. However, the big international players have located their Head Offices in Sydney—Microsoft, Apple, Google, and Facebook—and as much as they will control the critical mass of the future, including innovation spin-off, Sydney will have the ICT advantage. Sydney can also claim the generation of 60% of local tech start-ups.

The Australian media is overwhelmingly based in Sydney. Television includes all three commercial networks—Seven, Nine, and Ten—and both the Australian Broadcasting Commission and SBS. The ABC commands a pervasive national radio network, and increasing digital influence. It plays the lead role in the nation's current affairs reporting and discussion. It dominates children's television production.

The print media is much the same, with the two national companies, News Corporation and Fairfax, based in Sydney.

Sydney is home to the one national newspaper, *The Australian*, as it is to the daily *Australian Financial Review*. Australia's magazines have traditionally been produced in Sydney, where the Packer family's Consolidated Press has been the major force. Leading examples range from the long-running *Women's Weekly* and *Woman's Day*, to *Vogue* and *National Geographic*, and include lifestyle publications like *Better Homes and Gardens* and *Home Beautiful*. *Better Homes and Gardens* has the highest circulation of all, closely followed by *Women's Weekly*. Advertising is also predominantly sourced in Sydney. Three of the four large trade book publishers are based in Sydney.

The concentration of print and other media in Sydney might be expected to influence the nation's self-reflections. The ABC is often accused, by the rest of Australia, of being Sydney-centric, in violation of its charter. Commercial television too displays a southeast coast bias—little voice being heard from Darwin, Cairns, Hobart, or even Adelaide. But in the case of books, the location of the writer is much more important than that of the publisher. The West has gained a rich presence in the national imagination through Tim Winton's novels and stories. Similarly, David Malouf has projected some of the distinctive flavour of Queensland. It was not different when Henry Lawson lived in Sydney, and was published there, but set his stories in the outback.

There has been an intriguing shift too in political leadership. Post-1949, Prime Ministers came from Melbourne, where the Liberal Party had its strongest base—Menzies, Holt, Gorton, Fraser, and Hawke (his seat of Wills was in Melbourne). Since 1993, however, starting with Keating, Sydney has become the main Prime Ministerial source—home to Keating, Howard, Abbott, and Turnbull. In the other major sphere of civic life, the law, judges from New South Wales have been strongly represented in appointments to the High Court of Australia, notably since 1945. This reflects the quality of the judiciary in Sydney.

As part of the final deal that made possible the 1901 Federation of the colonies into the Commonwealth of Australia, New South Wales was granted the future national capital. Canberra is steadily turning into a satellite of Sydney, only 250 km distant (Melbourne is twice as far). The development of an economic and political power axis centred on Sydney is being further strengthened by the consolidation of Brisbane (including its Gold Coast and Sunshine Coast conurbations) as Australia's third major city.

Sydney Prime Ministers, starting with Howard, have tended to live in their home town, spurning The Lodge in Canberra—a choice facilitated by Sydney being alone of Australian cities in having its own Prime Ministerial residence—Kirribilli House. And there is a case to be made that Commonwealth funding of major national infrastructure projects has increasingly favoured Sydney, at the expense of the other cities.

Australia's creative life has been largely dual-city. The Sydney contribution includes the *The Bulletin* in the 1890s, which gave strident, formative voice to Australian nationalism, and in particular promoted, and part created, the culture of the 'bush'—exemplified in Henry Lawson stories and Banjo Patterson songs. The message was that Australia is distinctive, not just a diminutive extension of Mother England. Its own rugged vigour was exemplified in life in the Bush, a mythology to be adapted into the Anzac legend in 1915 (to be discussed below in Chapter 5).

Sydney artist Russell Drysdale took up the bush theme, in paintings starting in the 1940s, depicting tough wiry characters lounging in ramshackle, scorched outback towns. His best-known image is that of Henry Lawson's *Drover's Wife*—a gigantic ballooning figure stranded in an arid, featureless country wasteland, with pint-sized horse, wagon, and useless husband in the background. The story and its illustrative painting put the question: *Is she big enough to withstand the bleak, menacing agoraphobia of the Australian outback—stark contrast to the lush verdancy of Sydney?*

Patrick White, arguably the nation's one novelist of the first rank, and its only literary Nobel Laureate, was from New South Wales, and lived for the later decades of his life on Centennial Park in Sydney's Eastern suburbs. He provided a vivid picture of Sydney outer suburbia in his own favourite novel, *The Solid Mandala*. His epic masterpiece, *Voss*, counterpoises the soft civilised veneer of Sydney town with the scorching untameable expanses of the demonic outback.

The emergence of an Australian film industry of high quality in the 1970s was largely based in Sydney. Peter Weir continues to live there, as does George Miller. Weir directed such enduring film classics as *Picnic at Hanging Rock*, *The Last Wave*, *Witness*, *Dead Poets' Society*, and *Green Card*. George Miller has had an extraordinary and diverse career that includes the *Mad Max* quartet (the first filmed in Melbourne), *Lorenzo's Oil*, *Babe*, and *Happy Feet*. Baz Luhrmann (*Strictly Ballroom*, *Romeo and Juliet*, *Moulin Rouge*, and *The Great Gatsby*) is also a Sydneysider; as is Bruce Beresford (*The Club*, *Breaker Morant*, *Tender Mercies*, *The Fringe Dwellers*, *Driving Miss Daisy*, and *Mao's Last Dancer*). Taken all together this suite of films is a remarkable achievement.

The Australian Film Television and Radio School has been based in Sydney since its foundation in 1973, as has the National Institute of Dramatic Art (NIDA), since 1958. Both have been preeminent in quality and influence in the country. The AFTRS is the only screen and broadcast school in the world to cater for all of the specialisations under the one roof.

Sydney has predominantly served as the nation's classical music capital. It is home to the Sydney Symphony Orchestra, the Australian Opera, the Australian Chamber Orchestra, and the Sydney Conservatorium—generating a quantity, range, and quality of music hardly ever matched in the rest of the country. Moreover, the architectural presence of the Opera House has acted as a kind of coat-of-arms advertising Sydney music.

In the creative arts, there is a tradition of caricature that stands out. William Dobell painted portraits in the 1940s and 1950s of Joshua Smith, Helena Rubinstein, and Dame Mary Gilmore. More recently, Bill Leak published political cartoons in *The Australian* of Hogarthian insight and pungency, and with same quality of draughtsmanship as the eighteenth-century English master. His work served as the Sydney parallel to the Hogarthian genius of Melbourne's Barry Humphries.

The Sydney Olympics in 2000 was a national triumph, hailed as the best Games ever by much of the international press. The sparkling paradisiac look of the city, complemented by a golden climate, waved a magic wand across the event that charmed athletes, spectators, and international television audience alike. That the show ran with seemingly effortless smoothness and good cheer, with the aid of thousands of volunteers, just seemed a natural extension of the framing mood of benevolence.

Let me conclude with some Sydney snapshots from its own progeny. Donald Horne wrote in 1964: 'Sydney dreams of surfing, fishing, sailing, swimming in calm bays, lying stretched out in the sun, absorbing heat into the marrow. And it is now at last taking on some of the *feeling* of a great city, the first city in Australia to do so.'[82]

One of Sydney's illustrious sons, the international art critic, Robert Hughes, wrote with dark ambivalence about his home city: 'I wish they could tow Aus away, and let it sink!' Yet, in his history of the convict years, *The Fatal Shore*, he had speculated:

> *The visitor from England, arriving in Sydney in the 1820s, saw a bright prospect from the deck of his ship: Across the glittering blue of the harbour, under the immense clarity of the southern sky, a neat-looking town of freestone or white-washed cottages with shady verandas, their gardens marked off from one another and from the still-encircling bush with paling fences or clipped geranium hedges, their kitchen-yards "teeming with culinary delicacies".*[83]

Clive James was typically generous, as he gestured late in life back to the fine first volume of his autobiography, *Unreliable Memoirs*, which recounted growing up very happily in the working-class suburb of Kogarah, near Botany Bay. In *Return of the Kogarah Kid*, James writes dreamily of Dawes Point, the park under the Bridge in the Rocks area:

> *Here I began and here I reach the end.*
> *From here my ashes go back to the sea*
> *And take my memories of every friend*
> *And love, and anything still dear to me*
> *Down to the darkness out of which the sun*
> *Will rise again.*

He also wrote of Sydney:

> *It is just*
> *That we, who learned to breathe the brilliant air,*
> *And first were told that we were made of dust*
> *Here in this city, yet went out across*

*The globe to find game, should return one day
To trade our gains against a certain loss –
And sink from sight where once we sailed away.*

4
CIVIC CULTURE

Australian cities would not have prospered as they have in a cultural vacuum. A city is a social and economic entity that depends for its vitality on inhabitants guided and sustained by their civic culture.

Everyday life is conducted within a tight web of shared modes of conduct and belief, reflecting a kind of 'collective conscience'.[84] In the Australian case, the citizens generally like the manners they encounter when they leave the privacy of their homes, and venture out into the public domain. I want to suggest that the nation's civic, or public culture has three leading components, reflecting the spirit of the people. There is an attachment to the nation's institutions and a respect for authority. There is a practical democratic temper, complemented by a desire for inclusiveness and a sceptical philosophical orientation. These qualities have a long tradition behind them. They have been extended in recent decades by a third quality, partly new: a culture of hard work—an Australian version of the Protestant work ethic.

Australia's civic culture is overwhelmingly an English derivative. In the formative nineteenth century, England provided the explicit blueprint for the building of institutions, and for the ethos new arrivals brought with them in their cultural baggage, which they then applied unselfconsciously to their new society. Claudio Veliz described Australia as an island off the coast of Sussex—an image that retains a significant degree of truth.

The social and economic order constitutive of the modern world rests on two foundations, the industrial revolution and parliamentary democracy—both were made in England. It was Australia's good fortune to be born from this seed. It meant that the institutions and civic habits at the heart of modern development were familiar to its settlers; those blueprints and customs were, so to speak, in the cultural blood. Reproducing them was, accordingly, relatively easy. Also, adaptations could be made from a base of confidence and strength. Australian prosperity over two centuries has been partly due to smart adjustment to shock, and skilful response to changing international circumstances—as argued by Ian McLean, in his economic history of the nation.

Architecture provides a vivid illustration of cultural continuity, for better and for worse. English house design was copied, even when it was clearly at odds with the new environment and its climate—the better off built large brick houses with small windows in Toorak, Mt Macedon, and Portsea, and in their equivalent suburbs in other cities. With some exceptions, like building on stilts in Brisbane to utilise air circulation to counter the heat, it wasn't until the 1950s that houses adapted to the new place began to appear—with large plate-glass windows, sliding doors, and spacious verandas. The non-availability of plate glass is not an excuse, as it was invented in the nineteenth century and used extensively in celebrated London buildings like the Crystal Palace and major railway stations. (Whilst the larger homesteads in rural Australia did include verandas, their rooms had smallish windows that rendered the interiors very dark.)

Australian institutions have, with hardly an exception, been based on the British model. The State and Federal Parliaments in their foundation took their cue from Westminster, with minor borrowings from the United States—notably, a written Constitution and a Senate as chamber of review. The Departments that service government were modelled on the London civil service. The legal system derives from the English common law, case law, and trial-by-jury tradition, including the nature and culture of the judiciary, the form of the courts and their hierarchies, and the reference to English precedents in deciding particular cases. In fact, having an English legal system may well, in itself, constitute a major economic advantage: the extraordinary prosperity of modern Hong Kong is in part due to the nature, stability, and independence of its English legal system.

In nineteenth-century Australia, banking and insurance began in British forms, with companies often starting as branches of an English parent. It was London capital in the second half of the nineteenth century that provided much of the funding for public works and buildings; and the colonies had immediate access to world best-practice technology, which was British.[85] Schools, public and private, were set up to mimic the English model; and the universities have evolved from English red-brick institutions. Newspapers appeared as British clones; the ABC was modelled on the BBC; the Australian security service ASIO was set up on direct advice from London; and so on. Nineteenth-century Australian towns (minus the gum trees and the bright light) could have been mistaken for British provincial towns like Bristol—in their layout, houses, gardens, and general aesthetics.

Equally, the civic disposition was Anglo. Attitudes to politics, administration, and community organization—that is, political culture in the broad—reflected the parent emphasis on common sense; balancing principle and circumstance; preferring compromise over hard-line, stubborn ideology; respecting the law and other public institutions, and private property; respecting the primacy of the individual, and his or her privacy; and with all conducted under a prevailing canopy of communal responsibility for the public domain.

It was British prudence in 1847 in not ceding property rights to pastoralists that made possible the breaking up of large land holdings two decades later. The opening up of middle-scale farming that followed would enable agricultural diversification that insulated Australia economically in periods in which wool prices were low. Here was a main reason that the nation did not go down the Argentina path—falling from leading world prosperity in the late nineteenth century to steady decline from the 1920s.[86]

South Africa demonstrates that it is possible to have Anglo institutions without the ethos. Conversely, it is hard to imagine the ethos without the institutions.

a) Respect for authority

Australians are strongly attached to their public institutions. The new Parliament House in Canberra, opened in 1988, soon became the most visited building in the country. There is overwhelming respect for the courts and the judiciary, as there is for the police. Regard for the political and social armature has translated into a high level of civic order and stability.

Shakespeare was in step with most of the West's leading political philosophers (including Plato, Machiavelli, and Hobbes) in regarding order as central to a healthy and successful polity. He speaks through Ulysses, in praise of 'degree':

> *O, when degree is shaked,*
> *Which is the ladder of all high designs,*
> *The enterprise is sick. How could communities,*
> *Degrees in schools, and brotherhoods in cities,*
> *Peaceful commerce from dividable shores,...*
> *But by degree stand in authentic place?*
> *Take but degree away, untune that string,*
> *And hark what discord follows....*
> *Then everything include itself in power,*

Power into will, will into appetite,
And appetite, an universal wolf,
So doubly seconded with will and power,
Must make perforce an universal prey
And last eat up himself.

Troilus and Cressida, I, iii, 101-124

Music provides an analogy. It is only when an instrument is mastered, as a result of a long labour of instruction and practice, that the performer is free to improvise and create on the instrument. Degree enables freedom. So it is with political orders: only from within a frame of rigorous stability and continuity may a society develop, innovate, and prosper. Hobbes put it more strongly in his famous phrase, that the consequence of lack of order and weak government is anarchy, which renders 'the life of man, solitary, poor, nasty, brutish, and short.'

Australians themselves may be conservative about their political institutions, but they are adventurous in taking to the new, as they do for example with consumer products—rapidly taking up new technologies like mobile phones, laptop and tablet computers, multi-media devices, and internet social sites. They are adventurous in welcoming migrants, in large numbers and from diverse backgrounds.

Political order is valued by the Australian people, and in extraordinary measure. Proposed changes to the Federal Constitution are virtually always rejected in referenda, even when they are quite trivial. In the most recent non-trivial case, a 1999 Referendum to turn Australia into a republic, the proposal was overwhelmingly defeated (in all States). Of the total electorate, 55% voted 'no' in spite of the blatant fact that retaining the Queen of Britain as Australia's Head of State has become an anachronism—with both economic and military ties to Britain having declined into insignificance. The slogan 'if it ain't broke, don't fix it' carried the day, suggesting that the people prefer a practical working order that they trust to the abstraction of logical clarity. Not for them are the elegant rational models espoused by the Enlightenment, models which drove the French Revolution. Royal visits continue to draw huge crowds and attract unrivalled public interest. By 2014, support for a Republic had sunk to less than 40% of the electorate.

It is hard to conceive of a more stable polity, anywhere in the world, and at any time in history. Many may not like a particular government, or a particular Prime Minister, but this does not shake their attachment to the encompassing system. The people like their political institutions as they are, and don't want to risk damaging them.

The Constitution has itself inbuilt conservative checks. It may only be changed by a referendum, which has to be supported by Parliament then put to the people. For an amendment to pass there must be a double majority: an overall national majority vote, and a majority vote in a majority of the six states.

Voting is compulsory, and at all levels of government in Australia. The people willingly trade a liberal democratic principle (the freedom of choice to vote, or not) to force engagement in the electoral process. Again, the people prefer practicality to principle, having developed an electoral system that is less swayable by special interest groups, one in which parties do not have to waste resources on getting people to the ballot box, and one which gives greater legitimacy to the party that wins government.

The Depression of the 1930s sparked no major social unrest, in spite of severely reduced living standards experienced by a significant proportion of the population—in 1932, 29% of trade union members were unemployed.[87] More broadly, the long and protracted economic stagnation of the half-century between 1890 and 1940 did not provoke serious social or political upheaval.

Australia would withstand, almost completely unscathed, the Asian financial crisis of 1997, which saw international confidence collapse and with it a flight of capital from the region that severely damaged all other economies except those of Singapore and Taiwan—Thailand, Indonesia, and South Korea were particularly hard hit. It did so because of international trust in the strength, reliability, and incorruptibility of Australia's financial, legal, and political institutions. The same held for the global financial crisis of 2008, although in this case booming mineral sales to China helped keep Australia out of recession.

The people's liking for order has received vivid recent illustration with border security. The leading issue in the 2013 Federal election was stopping the flow of uncontrolled immigration to Australia, care of people smuggling in often barely-seaworthy boats from Indonesia. Public opinion strongly supported the Government doing whatever was necessary to regain authority over the borders (and there were other motives, including xenophobia, behind the hostility to 'boat people'). Paul Kelly has put a thoroughly documented argument that from 1945 there has been an unwritten compact between the people and the government, that the people will support high levels of immigration (which they do reluctantly at times), as long as government is wholly in control of the borders.[88]

The people's liking for order is reflected too at the mundane level in clean streets, well-kept parks and gardens, and general municipal tidiness. This compares with the public squalor on display in countries in which low levels of civic identification prevail, where citizens claim in effect that the shared domain is not their responsibility—in some American cities, parts of southern Europe and Latin America, not to mention the Middle East and Africa.

b) Practical democratic temper

There is an easy, friendly informality in social relations, which political leaders try to ape when visiting shopping malls, schools, and factories. It links to the national ethos of giving everybody a 'fair go'. This temper was central to the Anzac legend, with extension there into a cheerful resilience under pressure—echoed today in volunteer organisations like the Country Fire Authority.

To open in sociological terms: the people have developed their own distinctive form of democracy. Alexis de Tocqueville stressed that the democratic form of political order depends for its success on three things. All concern the limiting of the power of elites, and especially governments. First, is the prevalence throughout the society of a flourishing culture of free associations—clubs and societies. They range from sports organisations to charities, from trade unions to churches. Second, there must be an independent judiciary. Tocqueville's third requirement is a free press, able to publicise abuses of power.

Australia has added a fourth. It is pre-eminent. The main check on capitalism, on its inherent tendency to favour the ruthless self-interest of those with economic and political clout, has been the people.

Talkback radio illustrates. The main shows in each city attract high listener ratings. They open up the political and communal issues of the day for public discussion—from the treatment of illegal boat arrivals to the building of road tunnels and new train lines, from drugs in football to the guilt of Schapelle Corby arrested in Bali for cannabis smuggling. John Howard, when Prime

Minister, made a point of using talkback radio to test community reaction to proposed policy, and sometimes changed direction in response to what he heard.

There was the major role played at the Sydney Olympics by volunteers. They came from all corners of the country and helped to cast an ethos of friendly informality over an event that social commentators had predicted would be remembered as the last global mega-circus, disintegrating in media sparks and scandal. What integrity, it was queried, could issue from a self-serving International Olympic Committee, evasive on drugs, and addicted to its own five-star touring?

The Sydney mood was reflected in crowds that responded to Eric the Eel, as he was warmly nicknamed, an African swimmer floundering last in the pool, with no more ability than those watching. It was underscored by Roy and HGs nightly television show, *The Dream*, becoming the great hit of the Games, overshadowing the national triumphalism of gold-medal ceremonies. When the IOC attempted to ban athletes appearing on the medal dais with replicas of Roy and HGs star creation, Fatso the fat-arsed Wombat, rather than the officially credited mascots, it was public opinion that made it retreat in embarrassment.

An increasing number of American competitors appeared on the Fatso show, confessing to having been bewildered by the humour, and the phenomenon, before becoming captivated. One quipped that late nights watching *The Dream* had cost him first place in his event. Another said he would value his souvenir Fatso pin higher than his own gold medal. One effect of the Games was growing opinion in the United States critical of some of its own athletes for their brashness. The tone set in Sydney had made nakedly competitive pride jarringly out of place.

The people led during the Olympics, the media followed—

megaphone rather than opinion setter. Under the surface the same is true for politics. Indeed, Australia has inverted the civic axiom of ancient Rome, which had counterbalanced power to the people with authority to the Senate.[89] Here, the people have kept the authority, while uneasily ceding power to government.

A treasure trove for reading the nation was the ABC television series, *Calypso Summer*.[90] It documented one of those times of subtle cultural change. The occasion was the extraordinarily successful visit of the West Indian cricket team in the summer of 1960-61—a team farewelled by half a million people crowding the streets of Melbourne. To select one incident: Richie Benaud, the Australian captain at the time, reports how during the Second Test in Melbourne he appealed when the cap of West Indian batsman Joe Solomon fell on his stumps, dislodging a bail. The umpire had no option but to give Solomon out—a decision applauded on the programme as correct by the great West Indian all-rounder, Gary Sobers. The rules are the rules.

Benaud recounts with wry, self-deprecating amusement how among the 70,000 present at the MCG that day there were only eleven who did not boo him. So much for one-eyed jingoistic crowds! It was the people who had educated their captain, defending the spirit of the game, its code of good sportsmanship. They were expressing their native hostility to letter-of-the-law bureaucratic controls. The older Benaud had also ingested the culture's distaste for bragging, posturing, and pride.

A singular theme in the nation's history has been care taken to avoid conflict. John Hirst has outlined a range of cases in which institutions were planned in their foundation—government schools to name one—so as to minimize the sectarian strife between Protestants and Catholics that had plagued Britain and Ireland. Following the First World War, a similar attention went into choosing words for remembrance occasions that would be acceptable to all faiths. A Returned Servicemen's League inclusive of all religions was one fruit. Australia, in its first decade as a nation, exhibited the same impulse when it set up a government-run industrial arbitration system, unique in the world, which successfully helped to limit conflict between workers and employers.[91]

Indeed, industrial arbitration was just one component in the Deakinite Settlement, which framed the nation's political economy. Linked with a basic wage, tariff protection, and controlled immigration it set the terms of government—to guarantee a decent standard of living for all. The people's ethos of a 'fair go' was thereby institutionalised after Federation. In the 1980s there was a further adaptation, in response to changing economic challenges: the building of an 'Accord' between the Federal Labor Government and the trade unions, which guaranteed a safety net for the worst off, and agreed minimum wage standards, in return for restraint in wage growth. (The glaring exception to a fair go in the Deakinite Settlement was early White Australia legislation, which restricted immigration along race lines, and sent a message to thousands of Chinese residents that they were second-class citizens.)

Australia has been far less culturally coercive than the United States. It has put less pressure on its citizens, new or old, to conform to uniform customs, from those of marriage to forms of public behaviour such as the patriotism of the 'American way'. It has offered liberty in the fuller practical sense of freedom of choice of everyday life. The most telling illustration occurred during the First World War when the people, at referenda, twice voted against conscription—Australia, unlike Britain, the United States, Canada and New Zealand, would not force any individual to fight for it against his will. Australia would develop this unique conjunction: on the one hand, compelling its citizens to express their opinion, through compulsory voting, on the other relying in all its dangerous encounters, from war to fire to surf, on volunteers. Almost half the troops at the Western Front had themselves opposed conscription.[92]

There is a manner in Australia, different to that met, say, in many parts of Britain. It may justly be called a democratic manner. Not only at the Sydney Olympics, but inside the local suburban ballet school on Saturday mornings, the tennis club, in pubs and restaurants, shops, even passing through Customs on arrival in the country, there is typically an openness, a willingness to engage the stranger. Going into shops, even on the street, the elemental human interaction is less governed by ritual predictability, or the platitudes of formality. There is some likelihood of an ironic twist, certainly a personal exchange in which the outcome is unclear, even testing. An effort is made—visitors from overseas comment on this, ranking Australian cities the world's friendliest.

Here we experience a type of public vitality, of warmth and interest in the nuances of everyday life, of making the most of them. Ordinary incidents—a lemon tree dead in the backyard—may be deepened by a saying—She's decided to turn up her toes. Many Australian jokes focus on the meeting of strangers, and their laconic, playfully jousting banter. The film *Crocodile Dundee* exploited this trait.

There is a zest for language. Three post-war expatriates who were to become very successful internationally—Barry Humphries, Robert Hughes, and Clive James—all made their name through their exuberant, wild, and inventive use of spoken English. They have attributed their relish for language, and their pleasure in playing with it, to their Australian background.[93]

In Roy and HGs Olympic comedy, respect for sporting feats was subtly filtered through a rational lens, which casts all sporting events as absurd—Greco-Roman wrestling came in for special ridicule. A major attraction of the show was the deeper undertone in its jocular conversation—engaging with the paradox that is at the heart of most intense human endeavour. It is the strange mixture of taking the activity, whatever it might be, with ultimate seriousness, with devotion, striving to complete it with godlike perfection, while realising that it is of its nature arbitrary and absurd.

These themes are present at the MCG during a packed One-Day Cricket Match, when the Mexican wave gets going, circling the ground. As it reaches the Members' segment it stops, giving way to booing, before taking up again, in rhythm, on the far side. The booing is good-natured, even affectionate, a way of saying we know there is some sort of social hierarchy in this country—differences of wealth, position and status—but don't imagine you are better. We are all here together, unified by the match, the experience, and being Australian. On display once again is the talent of the people for inclusiveness. On display also is the collective neighbourliness, which I have already mentioned, one that is forged by a shared event.

The same kind of collective neighbourliness follows natural disasters like bushfires and floods, manifest in outpourings of sympathy, in donations of money, food, and clothing, and in the volunteering of assistance. It followed in the wake of the Sydney Siege which took place in Martin Place in the centre of the city on Monday/Tuesday December 15-16, 2014. A disturbed individual corrupted by a culture of Islamist violence held eighteen ordinary citizens hostage in a café for sixteen hours before two of them were killed, as was he. In the days that followed, an impromptu memorial was built in Martin Place, as thousands left flowers, and kept vigil. The memorial seemed partly to reflect, in grief, that some kind of unacknowledged spirit of national togetherness had been poisoned; an innocence had been lost. Also, in the days that followed there was widespread communal effort to minimise any reprisals against Muslim Australians.

Anybody is welcome as long as they fit in. Australians report that they like living with diversity, and approve of multicultural individualism as long as people 'mix.'[94] The terms of 'fitting in' and 'mixing' are loose, with the host society exerting comparatively low levels of coercion on newcomers—although there have been periods of communal tension, over Vietnamese migrants in the 1980s, and over Muslims after September 11, 2001. The reality is that, in the last seventy years, the vast immigration of peoples from hundreds of different backgrounds has been overwhelmingly successful. The host society has, as human societies go, been welcoming and exceptionally tolerant of diversity. It has made it clear to newcomers from wherever they came that they would be treated as equals, free to practice their traditional customs, as long as they left their ethnic conflicts behind them. Groups with a history of bloody violence—Greeks and Turks, Serbs and Croats to name two—have learnt, as 'New Australians', that there is a better way to live together.

Social cohesiveness continues to be very strong. The Scanlon Foundation Survey in 2014 found that 92% of Australians reported a strong or moderate sense of belonging (66% strong; 26% moderate); 88% expressed pride in the Australian way of life; and 91% stressed the importance of maintaining Australia's way of life and culture.[95]

Footballer Ron Barassi gained exemplar status, in small part because of his surname. One dimension to the making of him a local star was as means to a self-congratulatory, 'pat on the back' confirmation that *We are inclusive and tolerant*. Similarly, Aboriginal athlete Cathy Freeman was granted iconic national status at the 2000 Olympics, in part as a symbol of integration. Less self-conscious was the euphoria in 1960, when the visiting West Indies cricketers became surrogate Aussies. Or, in 2014, when Chinese tennis player Li Na became a special favourite with the crowds at the Australian Open, on winning the women's title. All societies harbour potential hostility to people who are different, but on any realistic scale of xenophobia Australia would rank very low.

Inclusiveness is generalised social capital, in a period in which most of the traditional manifestations of social cohesiveness are in decline—membership of churches, trade unions, political parties, charities, and sporting clubs.[96] Since the 1980s, Australians have been less inclined to join formal communities. Indeed, almost all sports are under threat from declining club membership—for instance, more play golf every year, but fewer join clubs. New forms of association enabled by social media lessen the appeal of the fellowship provided by traditional clubs—younger generations feel less need for the club type of community.[97] Surf Life-Saving Clubs are one exception to the decline, as is the volunteer-staffed Auskick.

One tradition within the discipline of sociology focuses on the modern decline of social capital—the degree to which people socialise together—foreseeing a pathological increase in social fragmentation, individual isolation, and weakening communal ties.[98] But the preference for more diffuse modes of socialising—a more diffuse neighbourliness—may well mean that the sociologists' fears are largely unfounded.

At times, inclusiveness does not come of itself, and has to be worked on. Riots that broke out in 2005 at the beach of Cronulla in Sydney were not repeated, largely due to the strenuous conciliatory work of community groups (Surf Life Saving Club, local Council, the police, and some Islamic associations). Riots that broke out in English cities in 2011 were in notable contrast, sparking copycat looting and vandalism across the country.[99]

The exception to Australian inclusiveness has been treatment of the original inhabitants. The country houses in essence two peoples and two cultures, with problems of coming together that continue to loom as intractable. True, there are emerging signs of fraternity—highlighted in the popularity of a television series, *Redfern Now*, and pride and delight taken in Cathy Freeman, through the length and breadth of the society, chosen as national ambassador to light the torch at the 2000 Olympic Opening Ceremony. There is growing acknowledgment in the White majority that the Aborigines have not, in general, been treated well—and at times shamefully. British settlement was conquest, and there is no way to gild the often-brutal eviction of peoples from their traditional lands.[100] The distance between the two cultures remains, and with it the most severe challenge to the people's capacity for inclusiveness.

Australians are by nature sceptical. They are uneasy about pretensions, grand ideas, ideological enthusiasms, and idealism of any colouring from the religious to the political. They baulk at utopian thinking as pie-in-the-sky, and unworldly. They view fanatics as unhinged, even demented. The nation's paradigm virtuoso commentators—Barry Humphries and Chris Lilley—both mock the local with a mixture of biting edge and affection. So did Roy and HG. There is a long and distinguished satirical tradition. In recent times, the whimsical metaphysical satire of Michael Leunig contrasts with the barbed public commentary of Bill Leak and John Spooner. Kathy Lette has observed that Australians are sceptical but not pessimistic.[101]

Here, much has been inherited from the English gene, and adapted—minus the tensions of the British class system. The English are given to understatement and self-deprecation; their comedy is laced with self-mockery. Their political culture is typified by reticence. At the highest level, Shakespeare established a commanding tradition, embedded in the language, which itself exemplifies the dynamic possibilities of surface anarchy and subterranean order. It is as if the language itself has prompted one of the wisdoms of English political life, which is to minimise explicit codification. Customs, agreed practices, and gentleman's agreements reflect civic trust, and they are more amenable than written rules to adaptation to changing circumstances, and managing the sheer complexity of the social world.

Shakespeare leaves a broad view of the human condition, presenting its ambivalences and complexities with a worldly-wise scepticism, modest in judgment, with a regard for honesty and trust in the personal, firmness and good sense in leaders, and a liking for the bawdy and the ridiculous to soften the hardships and tragedies that bedevil normal life.

Australia's favourite sporting stars in recent times—tennis player Pat Rafter and golfer Adam Scott—can both be characterised by modesty, balance, self-deprecation, and mildness of manner. In this, they belong to the tradition of Don Bradman, Rod Laver, and the older Richie Benaud. Tennis champion Lleyton Hewitt displayed an on-court brashness that was never liked; as has Nick Kyrgios a generation later.

Australians share with most peoples a conservative inclination in relation to civic order and public security. Yet the nation's political satire can be merciless, as it was in classical Athens, and in England from the eighteenth century. There is a dynamic ambivalence on show here, for Australians are overwhelmingly respectful when meeting their politicians face-to-face. It is as if they assert an unwritten contract: we cede power to you and expect you to lead, using that power wisely, but any failings will be pilloried in public. You serve us, and don't imagine that elevates you to some higher human level. Roy and HGs' *Dream* played on the same ambivalence in relation to sport. The preference in satire is for good-humoured mockery rather than viciousness; for harsh lampooning rather than angry, bad-tempered vilification. Australians don't like extremes of mood or behaviour.

Let us return to the central question posed in this book, the cultural preconditions for Australian prosperity. The practical democratic temper exhibited by the people—stressing a fair go, inclusiveness, and scepticism—satisfies one of the main criteria for economic inventiveness and creativity. To a singular degree, it lays the ground for open and mobile links between different socio-economic groups and their customs. It predisposes the society to building fluid and porous institutions.

c) Work

Australia has been characterised in the past as the 'lucky country', with a casual, easy-going population whose attitude to work was of the slapdash, 'she'll be right, mate' mentality. The Donald Horne line was the norm amongst commentators of an earlier generation, holding that sport was the only activity that Australians took seriously; the one in which they did strive to excel. Australia was compared unfavourably with the United States over attitudes to work.[102]

There was also a common trade-union mentality antagonistic

to the rest of the society and its interests. It was displayed at its worst in regular strike action that took place during the Second World War, when the nation was under threat. The war effort was compromised by gas, rail, and munitions factory workers, to name a few, who downed tools during the height of the Battle of Britain. Australian soldiers heading north to fight the Japanese in New Guinea, whilst docked in Brisbane, looked helplessly down from their ship rails as waterside workers pilfered their provisions. American aircraft parts were deliberately vandalised by wharfies, as were radar sets, probably leading to the deaths of American airmen fighting the Japanese. Strikes continued throughout the war, reaching an extreme in 1945, with over 2 million days lost.[103] On display here was a malign tradition inherited from Britain.

The reality today is that the country is hard working, nearly full-employed, and prosperous. And trade union membership has shrunk to 15% of the workforce, with that overwhelmingly in the public service (40% of employees); only 10% who work in the private sector belong to unions. While some of the old corruption and thuggery remains, especially in the construction industry, many of the unions have modernised—a transformation that occurred mainly in the 1980s, driven by an alliance between Labor Prime Minister Bob Hawke, Treasurer Paul Keating, and ACTU Secretary, Bill Kelty. Some modernisation required forceful confrontation, as happened on the waterfront in 1998, with a resulting large jump in the productivity rate of loading and unloading containers.

Australians report high job satisfaction: males 7.6 out of a possible 10, females 7.7, figures that are constant through the period 2001-8, with no variation for age. They work long hours: men in full-time work averaging 46.3 hours per week in 2008; and women 42.5 hours. These are striking statistics. Moreover, the hours were not coerced: 60% reported being content with their working week.[104] Recent in-depth interview studies have confirmed high levels of satisfaction with work.[105]

The statistics imply that a cultural change has taken place in attitudes to work. A local version of the Protestant work ethic appears to have evolved and strengthened. Concurrently, the passion of Australians for gambling remains undiminished. *The Economist* ranked Australians as the world's leading gamblers in 2014 in terms of losses per capita.

The leadership of three gifted Prime Ministers has played a key role.[106] Robert Menzies centred his political rhetoric on the silent majority of modest, hard-working, decent, family-centred people who constituted middle Australia, and through projecting that ideal he encouraged the very virtues he was championing, proclaiming early on that 'The home is the foundation of sanity and sobriety'.[107] Bob Hawke responded to the stagflation of the 1970s, and the collapse of the Keynesian macroeconomic model, by removing industrial protection and internationalising the Australian economy, while leaving a 'safety net' for the least well-off. He thereby sent a message to an over-protected nation that you have to prove yourselves on the world stage and earn your keep; there are no sinecures; the age of featherbedding is over. He managed to modernise trade union attitudes and behaviour largely by means of consultation. The equivalent transformation in the United Kingdom, carried out by Margaret Thatcher from the other side of politics, required violent confrontations, and it provoked serious social unrest.

A third Prime Minister, John Howard, combined the messages of Menzies and Hawke to address what came to be known as 'aspirational voters', those in middle Australia who expected through the good Protestant ethic virtues of hard work and thrift to improve their lot. All three Prime Ministers had a strong intuitive feel for the mood of the vast majority of the people. They drew upon that mood, and helped shape it—in a rare example of moderate politics influencing culture.

Australian football provides a marker of historical change. There was, in the 1980s, still admiration among fans for the 'gifted amateur', the player who drank heavily, maybe smoked, trained slackly, turned up at the last minute for the match, and then nonchalantly kicked six goals. By the first decade of the twenty-first century this had gone, replaced by the highest accolades being granted to super-fit professionals, like Chris Judd of Carlton—players who work with Spartan tenacity and rigour at training.

Admiration for sporting excellence in the population at large feeds into expanding use of fitness centres, exercise regimes, and personal trainers. It is offset by rising levels of obesity.

Australians like things to work. They swung against the Rudd Labor Government in 2009 for its clumsy administration of a scheme of providing free insulation for home roofs—the 'pink batts scandal'. Popular television regularly exposes shonky builders. The public is critical of governments when there are inefficiencies over access to hospitals and when city ambulances take more than twenty minutes to respond to an emergency. Parents rebel against government schools when they regard them as mediocre, and are willing to spend up to $30,000 a year for private schooling. This is not just a small minority, with 35% of school students in Victoria in the private system, although a majority of those do attend the less expensive Catholic network.

Education is viewed as important for getting on. Parents will work longer hours, take extra jobs, and make major economic sacrifices for the sake of their children. Their ambition for advancement and prosperity across generations indicates a confidence that self-help will be rewarded; and a belief that their society offers comparatively high social mobility, a belief that becomes, in part, self-fulfilling. On display is a disposition that does not respond passively to incompetence or inefficiency; one that prefers active resistance over a resigned shrug of the shoulders.

The new work culture is not, in any obvious sense, an English derivative. Indeed, it has been commonplace since the 1950s for employers in London, the dynamic hub of the British economy, to prefer employing Australians, and because of their work ethic—this has held from lawyers, accountants, and architects to shop assistants and bartenders. Reciprocally, the general experience of Australians working in London has been shock at the perceived laziness of the English.[108]

In part, the work ethic is not new, but picks up an old attitude characteristic of Australians, that of 'having a go'. From the days when the bush was more central to the national psyche, adversity and setback was to be met by resourcefulness and improvisation—illustrated in the proliferation of home welded and wired farm equipment. The modern enthusiasm for DIY renovation may have roots here. The worst sin is not to try; and better to fail, or to appear foolishly clumsy, than not to have given it a go. The crowds at cricket matches shout players on: 'Have a go, ya mug!' And Shane Warne, the best leg-spin bowler ever to play the game, had as his motto: 'Never give up.' Warne's popularity as a personality with the Australian public, and in spite of a lurid private life, was in part due to his irrepressible upbeat cheerfulness and confidence—the loveable larrikin who, at the same time, was smart, worked hard at what he did, and executed it brilliantly.

The work ethic, by definition, makes an indispensable

contribution to the nation's economic exceptionalism. It also reflects it.

In terms of the key contributing factors to prosperity, the work ethic has been complemented by the symbiosis of multicultural immigration with Anglo institutional forms and customs (Hong Kong and Singapore provide illuminating parallels). Some kind of creative friction has resulted, reflected in the fact that the inhabitants of Australian cities exhibit two of the key interpretative concepts in migration theory: 'assimilation' to host Anglo traits and a 'melting pot' in which different characteristics and habits blend together to form a new entity.[109] One virtue of the English tradition has been to tolerate a rich diversity of custom and belief, as long as there is conformity to a core of shared values. In Australia, this has functioned exceptionally well, and has served as a model of partial multiculturalism. The popular terms 'fitting in' and 'mixing' imply the need for a nexus of shared social values, but beyond that almost complete freedom of personal life choice.

Where the creative friction has been absent, due to low multicultural immigration, as in the case of Tasmania, Anglo institutions and customs on their own have not generated economic dynamism. Poor political leadership may have acted as a compounding factor in the Tasmanian case. The Apple Isle has not produced a Menzies, a Hawke, or a Howard.

South Australia has also been inhibited by less diverse immigration than New South Wales and Victoria. Its capital, Adelaide, with only 15% non-Anglo population, has a much more one-dimensional look and feel to it. Its economy has been the weakest performer after that of Tasmania. But, South Australia has benefited from more visionary political leadership, fostering local industry, higher education, and very successful arts festivals. Adelaide is currently undergoing transformation, utilising its topographical advantage of being, like Melbourne, situated on a river, and one of modest width. It has adroitly redeveloped the Adelaide Oval—to the point that it now outdoes the MCG in terms of presenting football spectacles. It has built an architecturally-striking bio-medical and hospital complex; renovated its Conference Centre; and, with universities playing a key entrepreneurial role, is in process of rejuvenating the CBD. The South Australian Government is working to build the CBD population to 30,000 residents by 2020; and will remove stamp duty on commercial property completely by 2018, in a strategic move to encourage business investment. (Mind, in a rush to convert to renewable energy it has cursed the State with the highest electricity prices in the country.) Overall, Adelaide is striving to do what it can to cultivate a lively city ambience.

An aspect of creative friction in Australia has been the impact of waves of hard-working new immigrants—from Germans, Dutch, Italians, and Greeks in the 1950s (especially in building and construction), to Vietnamese in the 1980s (restaurants), and to a plethora of Asian backgrounds in the 2000s. Economic assimilation has been enabled by porous institutions, as for example in the relative ease of starting new businesses, from cafés to textile factories, to construction companies (compared with much greater bureaucratic regulation inhibiting new enterprise in Continental Europe). As a different example, admittance to the medical profession has worked on meritocratic principles, as illustrated by high numbers of Jewish doctors from the 1960s, and Asian ones from the 1990s.

We may conclude that, in considering the civic culture of Australia, high levels of multi-cultural immigration have played a vital role, in conjunction with Anglo forms. As the city footpaths and laneways, and with them the urban landscape, come to look more cosmopolitan, so too creative and entrepreneurial energies have been stimulated. Locals become more spirited than they would have been otherwise; more cheerful and adventurous.

Civic culture is a kind of public moral temperament that evolves over time and spreads through the population. My task here, in considering the Australian case, has not been to chart its origins, but to note its leading features as it developed during the second half of the twentieth century. A respect for authority, a strong attachment to institutional order, and an easy-going practical democratic temper, have combined with an ethos of hard work to build a crucible in which animal spirits are freer to buzz and to fizz.

5

THE NATION'S MYTH

The comforts of family, work, and leisure, whether suburban or urban, are not enough on their own to provide the good life. For pleasure in the everyday, there needs to be a framing story, or series of stories. Life requires interpretation; it requires a plausible narrative to give it meaning. In part, this has come from celebration of local life and its virtues, through such avenues as the family and community dramas that are staple to popular television. In part, it has come from grander narratives, one cluster of which paints the nation in epic colours.

Two and a half thousand years ago, the Greek philosophers Plato and Aristotle outlined four character virtues. The concept of the cardinal virtues endures as a handy gauge, and for measuring the temper of peoples. There is courage. There is moderation, or balance, an evenness of mood and reaction. There is justice, knowing what is right and fair. And finally there is practical intelligence, perhaps we would call it common sense. It is a capacity for thinking clearly given the problem at hand, thinking that is balanced, directed to determining the right course of action, and conducted with an independence from fashion and coercion that may require courage. The preceding chapter said a lot about this.

A people, to feel free to let their character virtues speak unimpeded, must be at ease in themselves. One of the leading symptoms of insecurity is a tendency to extremism, to fanaticism or fundamentalism. Peoples, like individuals, take flight into ideology, dogmatism, moralism, and ranting when they feel under inner threat. It is a leading mark of Australia as a political culture to have always and without exception been sceptical of idealism, hostile to extremists, innately drawn to the moderate, the sensible, and the unassuming. This parallels openness to existential questioning. It points to a fundamental security of being.

Not that such security of being has always been complete. The nineteenth-century colonies were settled by people who had uprooted themselves (or, in the case of convicts, had been forcibly uprooted) from virtually everything that was familiar—apart from their shared English language. They had flung themselves into a vast and alien land as far from home as they could travel, that distance vivid in the memory from the many months of perilous sea-voyage that it took to get there.

Remoteness was the defining condition of the new land, captured in images like the 'Never Never', suggestive of some ghostly place beyond known geography and time. Given the universal human need for familiarity of people and place, and for a sense of continuity and belonging, anomie was a constant psychological threat. On the Hume Highway, joining Sydney and Melbourne, it is common to see the homesteads for expansive farming properties built near the road, as if to signal anxiety about solitariness, a desperation to huddle within sight of any passing traveller. Fear of being lost in the seeming infinitude of the bush may lie behind the plethora of signposts that pepper Australian country roads. And, Australia's grandest literary epic, Patrick White's *Voss*, centres on the heroic explorer who pits himself against the terrain and climate of the vast and formless interior—a physical and psychological landscape from out of some mediaeval painting of hell—and loses. Geoffrey Blainey has stressed that while the physical mastering of Australia was fast, the emotional conquest was slow.[110]

Australia's equanimity is a mystery. Especially given the circumstances! After no more than a hundred years as a conglomerate of dependent colonies, safely nestling under mother England's wing, a fledgling nation establishes itself. It does so during the twentieth century, a century in the West typified by political upheaval and cultural disenchantment. This was the century in which the old European civilizations, from which modern Australia derives socially and culturally, became themselves uprooted. If they—steeped in the security of their own long traditions—turned themselves metaphysically adrift, if the parent lost confidence in its identity and direction, what hope was there for the child? It is hard to imagine less propitious conditions in which a young offspring society might find its own feet.

So how did it happen? The political philosopher Hannah Arendt put the problem for the United States—in her 1963 book, *On Revolution*. She asked how the new society had managed to find belief in itself—legitimacy—after breaking free from England in its War of Independence. In answer she posited that Americans turned the act of foundation itself into their anchoring authority. The *Declaration of Independence* and the *Constitution* became the sacred texts. The 'founding fathers' as they were grandly called—George Washington, Thomas Jefferson, and later Abraham Lincoln—had special powers attributed to them, those of immortal ancestors. Arendt argues that without this monumental act of higher self-justification the United States would, like most other new societies, have foundered in instability.[111] Yet Australia has not foundered in instability. Nor has it sought a myth of political foundation.

Further, Australia has not followed another American tactic in what sociologist Robert Bellah has termed 'civil religion'.[112] That is to cast itself as God's chosen people, selected for its virtue, and set a divine mission. In an age in which political authority could no longer be derived from church religion, this enabled Americans to shift the focus of worship to the nation itself. By contrast, Australian symbolism has never represented this country as a new Promised Land. None of its stories cast the people as singled out for favour by a guiding divinity. There is no Old Testament *mythos* that the nation draws upon in order to halo its doings.

Nor have we had the explicitly religious vision of some of America's earliest settlers, whose ambition was, having left the corruption of the Old World, to build Boston as Augustine's 'City of God', a divine city on earth, one in which goodness would prevail. There are no signs that Australia ever felt the need for such sanctifying ideals.

America, furthermore, has been far more persuaded by the Enlightenment belief in progress. Much of its energy has been directed by hope that confident free individuals, through intelligent planning and hard work, may build a material civilisation that will sustain human virtue and happiness. Australians have been far more sceptical, their hopes more modest. Whatever their deeper view of the human condition, it is not utopian.

Nor has Australia followed the classical Roman path in search of its legitimacy. The Romans centred their cultural world on the sacred hearth—the private home was the locus of stable being. Even gods were brought indoors, figurines to the patron deity placed respectfully in the hope of attracting divine protection for the household. While Australians have been deeply attached to their castles, usually with a carefully-tended garden out the back, they have changed them too casually and frequently for their tie to be that of the sacred hearth, at least in a literal sense.

The obvious first point to make is that early Australia did not need to create its own grand narrative, for it inherited the British national mythology, including the ideal of Empire. As an integral part of the wealthiest and most powerful Empire on earth—the geo-political strength at the time—it had less reason to question its own identity. In this, it was notably different from the United States, which faced an Oedipal crisis of political legitimacy after its successful War of Independence. Australia's separation from the 'mother country' was slow and painless, with Britain having at times to hurry the clinging child's independence.[113] Historian Manning Clark used to characterise Australia's formation by the metaphor 'blood on the wattle'—in truth, in relation to the gaining of independence, there was no blood at all, which in itself makes the story very unusual, and shared only by that of New Zealand.

Every culture, to follow the German philosopher Nietzsche, depends on a 'fixed and sacred primordial site'.[114] Indigenous Australians amplify a similar view in their notion of the Dreaming. The implication is that all cultures are—like their own—centred on a body of myths or archetypal stories. For culture to retain its vitality these eternal stories, dating from a long time ago, must be retold by each new generation.[115]

So what then is the Australian Dreaming? It must derive largely from the Western *mythos*, with its major roots in classical Greece and the Jesus narratives. If this were the case then we could expect charged stories of our own, mythically compelling ones tapping into the original sources, reworking them while drawing on their force.

There is one of the formative Western stories that has resonated in Australia through the last century, and in various modes. It is that of the hero.[116] Homer filled out the archetype in the beginning, in the figure of the great warrior, Achilles—his story told in *The*

Iliad, the book that became the Bible for fifth-century Athens. The Homeric hero is not just the greatest of all warriors, godlike in his form in battle, but one who gains dignity through suffering—tragic dignity in the face of death.

In reading Australia culturally, a single story carries the public imagination, and continues to do so—Anzac. The Anzac legend is rooted in the archetype of the hero. Australia Day, commemorative of first settlement, has never gained a scintilla of gravity. Nor has the history of Federation, which for all its display of vision and political skill lacks the attributes of mythic narrative.

Anzac as legend was to a significant degree the creation of one man, C. E. W. Bean, whose greatest legacy is his own first six volumes of the Official History of Australia in the World War. A man who saw most of the campaign at first hand writes his two volumes on Gallipoli with evocative timeless force, celebrating the mettle of the soldiers. They have claims as the Australian *Iliad*. He asks about the men:

> *What motive sustained them? At the end of the second or third day of the Landing, when they had fought without sleep until the whole world seemed a dream, and they scarcely knew whether it was a world of reality or of delirium—and often, no doubt, it had held something of both; when half of each battalion had been annihilated, and there seemed no prospect before any man except that of wounds or death in the most vile surroundings; when the dead lay three deep in the rifle-pits under the blue sky and the place was filled with stench and sickness, and reason had almost vanished—what was it then that carried each man on?*
>
> *It was not love of a fight. The Australian loved fighting better than most, but it is an occupation from which*

the glamour quickly wears. It was not hatred of the Turk.... Nor was it purely patriotism, as it would have been if they fought on Australian soil....

Nor was it the desire for fame that made them steer their course so straight in the hour of crucial trial. They knew too well the chance that their families, possibly even the men beside them, would never know how they died.... What was the dominant motive that impelled them?

It lay in the mettle of the men themselves. To be the sort of man who would give way when his mates were trusting to his firmness; to be the sort of man who would fail when the line, the whole force, and the allied cause required his endurance; to have made it necessary for another unit to do his own unit's work; to live the rest of his life haunted by the knowledge that he had set his hand to a soldier's task and had lacked the grit to carry it through—that was the prospect which these men could not face. Life was very dear, but life was not worth living unless they could be true to their idea of Australian manhood. Standing upon that alone, when help failed and hope faded, when the end loomed clear in front of them, when the whole world seemed to crumble and the heaven to fall in, they faced its ruin undismayed.[117]

There are notable amplifications of the legend. Only two works of public art in the country I know arrest the viewer with deep pathos. One is the Rayner Hoff sculpture in the Sydney Anzac Memorial of a young soldier crucified on his shield and sword. The other is the memorial to Weary Dunlop in his home town of Benalla in Victoria.

The Australian War Memorial in Canberra—another Bean initiative—has become a sacred place. It is the soul of the national capital, with visitors in their daily thousands passing through and gazing with hushed awe at the stories of gallantry and sacrifice, especially as retold through three-dimensional models of key battlefields. By contrast, the National Museum of Australia, five kilometres away, is a muddle of ill-told stories.

The presiding image at the Memorial is Will Longstaff's painting of the *Menin Gate at Midnight*. Spot-lit like a sacred relic in a blackened crypt, it shows a classical ruin, here mausoleum, set in the fields of Flanders near Ypres, all ground to devastated rubble and mulch by cataclysmic shelling. Across this gloomy night wasteland, like thousands of stalks of silver wheat in a lunar breath, move the ghosts of the soldiers. The painting echoes the cry of bereaved mothers after the war, when a memorial was erected in their local town or suburb. At last they could find some peace. For while the bodies of their sons, lost in action, were buried in some foreign soil, known only to God, their souls had finally been brought home—to rest.

Once a memorial is clothed in such gravity we know that Dreaming is awake. This place is no longer the Never Never. The tragic *mythos* of the West consecrates the ground, a voice awakened out of its Dreaming slumber every Anzac dawn as the bugle sounds the Last Post. The mournful cry joins those who rise to the new day with the shades of the long departed outside the Menin Gate.

The mood of Longstaff's elegy is reminiscent of the final two chapters of *The Iliad*, both centred on funerals. Indeed the whole Anzac tradition has eerie classical Greek affinities. Arendt links American foundation back to the ancient Roman blueprint. Australia's sources are Greek.

Australia's Exceptional Prosperity and the Culture that Made It

Why Gallipoli? The place is arbitrary in relation to Australia, even geographically absurd. The Dardanelles lie on the other side of the world, with no British traces, and the military campaign was a failure. And yet! From the heights of the Anzac objective on landing can be seen in the distance to the south, on a clear day with the help of binoculars, the ruins of the ancient city of Troy. Troy was the site of *The Iliad*. It is as if Australia had deliberately chosen its own sacred origins within breathing proximity to the birthplace of the West.

The tens of thousands of First World War memorials, built throughout Australia in a tidal wave of unparalleled public tribute, are in their design and their inscriptions rigorously classical. Statuary in towns and suburbs, as Ken Inglis' definitive study makes clear, is mainly of diggers or obelisks.[118] By far the grandest monument, the Shrine of Remembrance in Melbourne, derives from two ancient Greek temples. An unconscious drive to keep out Christian motifs seems to have been at work. The sacrificed youth in the Sydney memorial is the exception, yet not, for Anzac Day marches avoid it, gathering at dawn at the Cenotaph in Martin Place, before moving to the Domain.

In all of this there is one major *midrash*, or adaptation of the classical Greek hero. Australia does not celebrate Achilles himself, the great individual—or, to switch to the most powerful modern American reworking, the John Wayne film persona, or its local equivalent. Australia has remembered the men, and above all their character, not individuals. It has remembered the people, with the unknown soldier as national hero, one of Longstaff's ghosts. There was no statue to any individual soldier before 1936, when Simpson was unveiled in Melbourne. Even then the work is titled: 'The Man with the Donkey', and what is honoured is selfless service—not warrior prowess.

The same is true of the one subsequent war hero to be revered by the nation—Weary Dunlop.[119] A surgeon, his story combines superhuman courage with compassion. The Christian image of the suffering servant seems to have entered the national consciousness by the back door, avoiding the churches, journeying via classical Greece. Simpson and Weary are the only two individuals honoured in sculpture at the Canberra War Memorial.

Bean ends his first volume with the question of what carried each man on, when realising that he had been cast into some godforsaken Turkish wilderness without food or sleep, the dead and wounded all around, the cause seemingly hopeless. Bean's answer was character.

One individual national hero stands above the rest. Don Bradman's status depended originally on his class as a batsman—everyone else who has ever played the game of cricket ordinary by comparison. But 'The Don', as cricketers from both teams during the Calypso Summer referred to him, a title in itself rich with associations of chivalry, but also informal, intimate; the Don came even more to embody an Australian character ideal. The voice was indicative. A touch nasal with Australian vowels, its undertone slow with reticence and modesty, it yet resonated with a buoyant high-pitched impishness, the words carefully chosen yet almost always combining a touch of humour with serious intent. C. D. Kemp put it: 'He was one of us but distinguished.'

Richie Benaud recounts how at the end of the tied First Test in Brisbane he was distraught at having let the game slip away. Bradman, as Chairman of Selectors, came up to him in the rooms with a huge smile on his face and told him not to worry: 'You will find that this is the greatest thing that's ever happened to the game of cricket.' West Indians recall with delight, and some awe, how the Don would sit with them during matches and openly discuss tactics. They attribute an extraordinary, completely out of character Wes Hall performance with the bat, to one of the great man's ribbings. Three decades later Conrad Hunte would refer to Australia as his spiritual home.

It was the Don's initiative to name the trophy that will forever mark Australia–West Indies cricket after the visiting captain, Frank Worrell. Indeed, Bradman's constant presence throughout the series sets an image of benevolent, far-sighted, and vigilant yet understated authority evocative of the national ideal.

The choice of Australian of the Year in 1999, on the millennium cusp, and in the decisive year for the Republican Movement, was the immediate past cricket captain, Mark Taylor. At a first glance, he was an odd type of modern ideal, portly of frame, not stylish of manner or speech—indeed quintessentially unmodish. He quietly, almost surreptitiously over the years, gained the respect of the cricket-watching public. They came to realise that he was impossible to rattle, even when his own disastrous form with the bat became a national talking point.

'Tubby' Taylor could be typified as the man who is untroubled about his identity. Taylor's character included down-to-earth practicality, a shrewd tactical intelligence geared to instinct and flair, and a seemingly unflappable confidence in his own judgment. Team-mates said that however depressed their spirits, however badly the team was doing, ten minutes talking with him, and they felt buoyant again. He was the opposite, in other words, of the 'neurotic', typified by Freud as someone who makes other people nervous.

The maniacally gum-chewing, plain speaking, irrepressibly good-spirited captain, courteous in a democratic rather than aristocratic manner, was keen on cricket tradition. So much so that, on one occasion in Pakistan, when himself on 334 not out, exactly Bradman's record score for Australia, Taylor declared the innings closed. Who was he to overtake the great man! This act flabbergasted local players and commentators, not used to individual sacrifice—and here in reverence, championing a national ethos.

Mark Taylor had instituted the practice of the whole team wearing the 'baggy green cap' in the first session of every Test Match, in spite of resistance from some of his senior players. In backs-to-the-wall situations he would say: time to don the *baggy green*. The nation's cricketers had been first to wear the green and gold colours—in England a century earlier, pre-Federation. Taylor also made it known at his retirement that he wasn't keen on constitutional change.

The need for the hero is sustained in modern sport. The nation's attachment to that segment of its life, above any other apart from family, is more than to an exciting communal pastime. Most of its serious conversations about the character of men and women under pressure are sporting ones. There is likewise a ready lineage back from contemporary cricketers through the Don to the Anzacs, paralleled by each Country Fire Authority volunteer, who will usually double up as a member of the local footy team. And the nation's esteem for the twin role of hero and volunteer is patent in the freest of its social spaces, the beach, in the figure of the surf lifesaver.

As a sociological generalisation, the grander articulations of national identity are projected, on one front, through heroes, stars, and exemplars. Post-war, sport played the major role in Australia.[120] The Bradman era set the scene, with the 'Invincibles' team that he captained triumphing in England in 1948. In a comparatively minor key, Walter Lindrum had towered over world billiards in the way Bradman towered over cricket, until his retirement in 1950.

The sporting pinnacle came with the 1956 Melbourne Olympics, in which Australia finished third in the national medal tally, behind the United States and the U.S.S.R. In the same period, Australia dominated tennis, winning the Davis Cup fifteen times between 1950 and 1967—repeatedly beating the Americans. In golf, Peter Thomson won five British Opens. The 1950s ended with the Calypso Summer series, opening with a tied cricket test in Brisbane, which attracted unprecedented enthusiasm, even euphoria throughout the country.[121]

1950s sport played a role in the separation from Britain—proving the nation could stand on its own feet and compete in the international world. The implied story was one of virility and excellence—of manhood. These were same terms with which Anzac had originally been celebrated, thirty years earlier, as proof that the men of the new nation were not of inadequate human stock (as descendants of convicts), but were equal to those from the home country. The first Anzacs had gone further, demonstrating superiority in physique, in mental independence and toughness, and as soldiers.[122]

Australia's own Oedipal separation sequence had opened with the fall of Singapore in 1942—the critical parallel, if in a much lower key, to America's War of Independence. Britain could no longer be relied upon to protect Australia from invasion. After 1942, the hitherto taken-for-granted axiom that if Britain was at war, then so too was Australia, would never again be held.

The fall of Singapore was followed by an immediate switch to the United States as the nation's principal ally. And post-war, the rising influence of American consumer and popular culture confirmed the new allegiance. The Oedipal symbolism had changed. For, the United States did not bear any parental attributes, being seen more like a bigger, elder brother. Indeed, it had sprung from the same parent, if over two centuries earlier.

The 1960 Calypso Summer symbolised the demotion of the Ashes as identity-defining cricket, with the West Indies becoming, for the moment, Australia's favourite foreign team. The disappearance of the teaching of British history in schools followed; as did the replacement of British currency with a decimalised dollar. The Ashes has subsequently regained popularity, but with the enthusiasm more mellow, it now standing as one among many sporting highlights. The Oedipal separation was completed in 1973 when Britain joined the European Economic Community, cancelling preferential Commonwealth trading arrangements—a move that was far more traumatic for New Zealand than for Australia.

In recent decades, there have been many signs of the diversification of the sources of national identification. Sport no longer holds a monopoly. The most professional, best-managed, most prosperous, and most culturally-creative sport in the country is Australian football, at the top AFL level. If Australia were preoccupied with world comparisons, the AFL would languish as an amateurish provincial oddity. The world game, soccer, has failed to become a major presence—with the player quality mediocre, game attendances poor, and management lacklustre. The success of the Australian Institute of Sport, which was set up after an embarrassing performance at the Montreal Olympics in 1976 (Australia won no gold medals), shows that the country can produce sportsmen and women of top international quality, if it puts its mind to it.

Further evidence of the decline of sport nationalism is illustrated in low public interest in professional golf, in spite of the country having had two players ranked in the top ten in the world in 2012, 5 in the top 50, and 10 in the top 100; and 2 in the top 4 in 2014, including Number 1, Adam Scott; and the Number 1 again in 2015 and 2016, this time Queenslander Jason Day. The Australian Tennis Open, in spite of locals no longer proving competitive, has become ever more popular (measured by attendance and television ratings). Australian fans seem to have happily found favourites among the best international players.

Whilst sport does continue to attract some national enthusiasm—Cadel Evans was lionised in 2011 after winning cycling's peak event, the Tour de France—it has been joined by other life spheres. A string of actors have succeeded in Hollywood, led by Olivia Newton-John, Mel Gibson, Nicole Kidman, Russell Crowe, Geoffrey Rush, and Cate Blanchett. Likewise, pop musicians have achieved top success on the international stage, led by Olivia Newton-John, the Bee Gees, AC/DC, INXS, Kylie Minogue, and Nick Cave. Maverick figures like nature-superman, come television-entertainer Steve Irwin have entered the national imagination. A broadening of the culture has also brought, for instance, women leaders into the public eye, such as a former CEO of the Westpac bank, Gail Kelly, and former Governor-General Quentin Bryce.

On a quite different front, a two-hour Channel 9 television documentary on the December 2014 Sydney Siege was both deeply moving and strangely uplifting. It was uplifting mainly because of the conduct of two heroic 19-year old students, Jarrod Morton-Hoffman and Fiona Ma. Their actions during sixteen hours of terror were calm, smart, and courageous; and their reflections, in the later television interview, were eloquent, and engagingly mature.[123]

In terms of the grander mythos, adulation of exemplary individuals is being complemented by a new phenomenon: pride in national achievement. The national economic success of the last quarter-century is central: withstanding the 1990s Asian financial crisis, the 2008 Global Financial Crisis, and remaining largely untouched by a European sovereign debt and banking crisis. On another front, there is the impressive scale of vast, 'can do' mining projects, from iron ore, to coal, to liquid gas—continuing a tradition of patriotic interest in national development, reflected in the 1960s in popular tours of the Snowy Mountains Hydroelectric Scheme, and later in visits to the New Parliament House in Canberra.

It is too early to be entirely sure about the depth of emerging traces of self-confidence, the contours of their expression, or their lasting impact. One indicator of confidence is continuing public support for high levels of immigration in the immediate post-boom years 2014-17, in spite of higher unemployment levels and greater job insecurity. But this confidence would be tested by a prolonged period of economic recession. As a cautionary precedent, it was only five years on from a London journalist's admiring moniker 'Marvellous Melbourne' that the descent began into that city's long and confidence-shattering economic depression of the 1890s.

In geo-politics, there is pride in an unprecedented friendliness with the United States, which began with a close personal relationship between John Howard and George W. Bush. The reality is that Australia has become a more significant player on the world stage, with location in Asia transformed from a liability—for a middle-size Western power—into an opportunity.

Paradoxically, while the pantheon of men and women admired by the nation has diversified, the Anzac legend has, over the last quarter-century, found renewed vigour, and spontaneously from within the social fabric. As if coinciding with the passing away of the last of the men who fought in the Great War, attendances at the Anzac Day Dawn Services surged around the country, and at the morning parades. In 2016, 70,000 attended the 5-45am Dawn Service at the Shrine in Melbourne; 30,000 in Canberra; and an amazing 1200 gathered for a new service in the pre-dawn light in suburban Dingley. In the main cities, later in the morning, crowds of 200,000 or more assembled to watch a march-past of former soldiers, sailors, airmen, nurses, and their descendants. Simultaneously, pilgrimages to Gallipoli became popular, especially among a younger, backpacker generation, with crowds of 10,000 gathering every April 25th at the site in the Dardanelles. The Dawn Service in Canberra in the centenary year 2015 attracted hundreds of thousands, packed along the boulevard running from the Memorial down to the lake, deeply moved in the half-light as the bugles were accompanied by birds in full song.

Anzac is confirming its status as the nation's single and presiding national myth by invigorating other pursuits, like an Australian football match started in 1995, which weaves rituals of quasi-sacred remembrance in with the game, creating an aura of reverential gravity. It has become the biggest match of the season apart from the Grand Final, with tickets sold out weeks ahead. This annual football contest underscores the strange fact that ritual is the main narrative vehicle for the Anzac story.

The Anzac revival has coincided with the new national confidence, and the third economic boom in the nation's history. It was as if there had been a cultural interregnum between the decline of British identification in the 1950s, and 1990, filled in part by youth hedonism in the 1960s, brief political idealism that flared around Prime Minister Gough Whitlam in 1972-3, and an efflorescence of national film, television, and drama through the 1970s—writers, directors, and actors combining to tell vernacular Australian stories. The 1970s was, at the same time, a decade of economic stress, which included stagflation and high unemployment. The nondescript 1980s followed.

Alternative myths to that of Anzac have failed to catch the national imagination. The leading nineteenth-century idealisation of Australian character and identity came in the form of the 'bushman', a man typified by his egalitarian temper and the value he placed on mateship, and by his affinity for his natural home, the bush. The legend was lapsing, for want of relevancy in an urban society, already by 1958 when Russel Ward celebrated it in his book *The Australian Legend*. Don Watson has recently explored the reality of the Australian experience of the bush, both less Romantic and more powerful, dark, and profound—in his magisterial cultural and social history *The Bush* (2014).

The other potentially mythic heroes of the nineteenth century—notably the explorers, bushrangers, and the pioneers—never generated a tradition akin to the American Western (apart from the isolated instances of *Voss* and Sidney Nolan images of Ned Kelly in armour, not to mention a few mediocre bushranger films).

In the political sphere, splutters of socialist idealism fizzled on a long litany of international catastrophes, led by Stalin's trials and the Soviet Gulag, Mao's cultural revolution, Cuba's economic stagnation; and locally by the failure of Whitlam followed by the centrist economic pragmatism of the Australian Labor Party under Bob Hawke.

Robert Hughes in 1987, responding to his nation's need, as he saw it, for a foundation myth, published a monumental attempt to answer the call—*The Fatal Shore*. His suspicion was that the facts about the convict era had been suppressed, and because the nation's formative experience was one of evil, oozing a stain across the fabric of society that was too shameful to admit. He refers to Australia's Gulag, draws a parallel with America's Civil

War, and his title picks up imagery of hell which some convict songs had painted. Hughes sought to deepen the Australian story by sourcing it in the dark waters of original sin and Biblical Fall.

But Hughes' enterprise failed totally, and because of the author's respect for the facts as he found them. The truth was that the convict experience—with some exceptions like penal life on Norfolk Island—was benign, given the nature of the times. Most of the convicts, when they were given the choice of returning to Britain, chose to remain in the colonies. Likewise, most of the men who had been imprisoned on hulks in England, and sentenced to transportation, wanted to be sent to Australia.[124] The convict experience anticipated that of most who would later travel from Europe to settle in Australia, driven mainly by the motive of improving their material circumstances: they were happy in the comparative prosperity of the new world as they found it.

As if by some kind of cosmic irony, it was at the very time of the release of *The Fatal Shore* that the Anzac legend began its revival. Erupting from the nation's collective unconscious, unprompted, like every true myth, projecting its themes as it were across the gulf of the River Styx, for its matter was now separated by death from the live actors, ferried by Longstaff's ghosts, it was freed finally to become legend. Its manner of rebirth confirmed that authority lay with the people, not with the State, nor with literary and intellectual culture (some intellectuals continued to express frustration at the myth's survival, and others penned a counter-myth of Gallipoli as British incompetence and betrayal). Anzac was a myth of the people, for the people, born from within the people. Moreover, its nature had this time become clear: it was the nation's creation myth.

This was a story to be told through ritual and illustrated by sacred relics housed at the Canberra War Memorial. It seemed to require more active and communal participation from its pilgrims than to a written or spoken narrative. That the Dawn Service had emerged as the presiding rite indicated that the people had become engaged in national remembrance and mourning on an epic scale—at an annual funeral staged across the country (again, an echo of Homer). As the bugle sounds the new day (not the completion of the old one), every April 25th, the gravity of the Australian mourning rises aloft in the early light, transmuted into awe. The most powerful of archetypal themes—death and its transcendence—was being tied back to creation, with tragic pathos the source of its vitality. This is a creation myth focussed on sacrifice, a collective journey down through the underworld, drawn by the silver thread. The men had not died in vain, for their sacrifice had given birth to a nation, one that could be proud of itself, and one that gained legitimacy from their courage.

Anzac was backed by mythic history, with the caveat that Bean's six volumes are themselves now virtually unread, except in contemporary midrash, with books on Australia's role in the Great War, including biographies of soldiers, streaming out each year and generally selling very well—Les Carlyon's *Gallipoli* (2001), for instance, has sold 60,000 in hardback, and well over 100,000 in paperback.

The story itself hardly needed telling, for it was known. It coursed through the cultural bloodstream, from 700BC when Homer provided its form, which had then resurfaced repeatedly through the long history of the West in myriads of adaptations. That form was austere, spare, and simple—quite unlike America's foundation legend with its complexity of content and character, and its need to proselytise. Accordingly, the Australian legend did not generate great poetry (no Wilfred Owen or Siegfried Sassoon), great novels (no *All Quiet on the Western Front* or *Regeneration*), or epic films. It is worth noting that America's greatest myth-forging film director, John Ford, could never manage to tell a significant story about the subject that was closest to his heart, his nation's tragic Civil War. His one full-length feature film on the Civil War, *The Horse Soldiers* (1959), is one of the weakest of his maturity. Likewise, Peter Weir's *Gallipoli* (1981) is out of character for the director, being pedestrian and cliché-ridden.

And, Anzac continued to evade giving prominence to exemplary individuals, even though there were numerous worthy candidates, led by General John Monash. Its resistance to telling individual stories was in keeping with an antipathy to the literary mode. The people had chosen it this way, in contrast to their celebration of sporting stars.

A twenty-four year old, son of a Polish post-war migrant, observed in 1999:

It's our national day of pride. People don't look like they are searching for anything during the day.... They look like they have found it.

Somehow Anzac worked. Creation myths come in odd forms. Aphrodite, goddess of beauty and love in Greek mythology, was born of the sea, from the foam issuing from the genitals of castrated Uranus. And Athena, goddess of wisdom and just war, was born, fully-grown and armed for battle, out of her father's split head—he was Zeus, king of the gods. Creation is intimately tied to rebirth, and to initiation motifs. Creation myth narrates the rite of passage from the chaos of embryonic form to maturity.

The Australian initiation is from pre-nation formlessness into timeless gravity. The original state was back-of-beyond, Never Never, and dependency on Mother England via the cultural umbilical cord. Today's rite of remembrance evokes a mood of reflection, and recognition of the founding reality that our way of life and its prosperity did not spring fully-clad out of nothing. On Anzac morning the supplicant is tuned in to the mournful bugle, and arrested by the hues of first light. He or she is being connected with things bigger than their lives, rugged up as they are in daily cares and pastimes. Between 1915 and 1918, 60,000 men sacrificed themselves to something higher than living, enshrining a collective spirit of invincibility that bestows the gift of authority on the people.

* * *

There is a conundrum. In Australian Dreaming *mythos*, the hero figure appears to stand virtually alone. The hero's pervasiveness signals how one-dimensional a legacy it represents. Where are the other stories of tragic suffering, of Passion, of the metamorphosis out of fallen worldliness, of love, of the gaining of poise of spirit? Where are the mother, where are other trajectories of vocation, of fate, and even stories of evil? Women have largely been absent.[125]

Which takes me to archetypal narrative's other domain. The antipode to the epic is the domestic story, which projects the archetype of home and family. Here, women have been predominant.

Suburban life in the 1950s found its legitimation in television dramas like the American series *Father Knows Best* and *Leave it to Beaver*. Family life in the suburbs was idealised as the sacred core of the good life, with its cardinal virtues in domestic love, loyalty, security, decency, modesty, and community service. The mother was the centre of gravity, the sun around which the rest of the family orbited. In this world, father did occasionally know best, but mother was the emotional heart and soul, the source of vitality and belief—and she often knew best.[126] In Australia, the suburban ethos was reinforced in long-running radio series such as *Blue Hills* (actually set in a country town), in magazines like *Women's Weekly* and *Woman's Day*, in advertisements, and in the popular press.

Home as a key locus of meaning has not changed in essence since the 1950s, and in spite of major shifts in patterns of employment, with a much higher proportion of women working, the two-income family becoming the norm, with greater sexual equality in the public sphere, and with much greater consciousness of patriarchal prejudices and discriminations. Home remains the 'haven in a heartless world', to draw on Christopher Lasch's book-title phrase from 1975. Australians spend a steadily increasing proportion of their wealth and incomes on buying and renovating the family home.[127] The enduring centrality of the home is illustrated on television, by the top ratings attracted by renovation shows like *The Block*, and DIY shows like *Better Homes and Gardens*. And politicians try to gain public appeal by being photographed with babies, sitting talking with school children, and expressing concern about how cost-of-living increases will impact on families. The power of the 1950s ideal of the family is illustrated in the enduring popularity of American versions of Christmas songs from that period, songs like Jingle Bells, Rudolf the Red-Nosed Reindeer, and Silent Night.

The fact that the Australian birth-rate remains high by Western standards itself indicates continuing belief in the family. And, although divorce rates rose rapidly after the 1970s, the nuclear family has continued to flourish: for instance, it remained the case that 77% of children born between 1981-85 spent all of their first 15 years living with their biological parents.[128]

The most highly charged and prominent stories told in popular culture—press, talk-back radio, and television drama—depict harm being done to children. They range from abduction, parental abuse, and paedophilia, to brutal night assaults on innocent teenagers. These stories draw upon a universal moral law, that of the protection of the innocent. Behind the horrified shock and moral outrage that they evoke, an implicit core value presides, that of the sanctity of the family. Any violation of it is judged as a kind of desecration, a crime against what the community regards as most holy. In these stories, in effect, a national mythology is being fortified. A Royal Commission into Child Abuse, which began hearings in 2013, received wide media coverage—it had been set up by the Gillard Government, and was regarded across the political spectrum as that Government's greatest achievement.

Even in the more upper-middle-class milieu of the ABC, a 2013-14 television series *The Time of Our Lives* covertly proselytised the family home as earthly paradise (or, at least, the crucible for the good life). The heart of that home was, as ever, the mother, she who bestows an earthy glow. In the series, those who damage the family were judged harshly, both implicitly and explicitly; the family unit was defended by older generations; and the core family in the show was warmly celebrated, if in more subtle tones than *Father Knows Best*.

The domestic ideal permits a role for free will and freedom of choice, in contrast with the fatalism of the grander mythology sourced in Anzac. Within the human order, Australians can be adventurous—rather than cautiously conservative. The family home is changed frequently, especially compared to standard European practice. There is great interest in renovation, and especially in do-it-yourself renovation; in buying model homes, which can be fitted out and furnished to suit the style and needs of the particular family; and to shifting whenever families grow, or contract, or to suit different phases in the life-cycle. For instance, city couples on retirement may sell the large suburban home where they have dwelt for most of their adult lives—the home full of family memories—and move to an inner-city apartment. That the home is to be created and moulded suggests some optimism about the freedom of individuals to shape their own destinies.

The endurance of the home as ideal is not peculiar to Australia. Cormac McCarthy, America's finest contemporary author, in his Border trilogy written in the 1990s (*All the Pretty Horses*, *The Crossing*, and *Cities of the Plain*), projects through his leading characters the virtues of innocence, grit, and integrity, while those characters dream of home and family, and one strives to make it a reality. The domestic yearning is all the more striking here, in that McCarthy's literary genre is singularly un-domestic, that of the Western.

The Australian national myth has come in two forms, one epic and the other domestic. It is not possible to determine which is the more significant, attributing valencies. The ways stories reverberate in the deep substratum of individual being is mysterious. What we can be sure of is that both forms become more vivid during times of crisis, like bushfires and floods. Anzac resonates in stories of fire-fighters, other rescuers, and those who had close shaves; and the domestic archetype is animated in the focus on homes burnt or flooded, and family members dispossessed or killed. To continue the Greek associations, the patron deity of classical Athens, Athena, had a dual persona: the grandeur of the role of goddess of just war and goddess of wisdom, combined with a domestic role as guardian of women and the hearth.

How has the rise of the city impacted on the national mythology? Home and family have, from the 1950s, been promoted as a suburban ideal, enabled by the evolution of the Australian city. And, this has itself extended, in the last quarter-century, into the urban milieu. The cities have themselves developed, in part, as supporting milieus for families; with the home ideal playing its own role in driving that development. Reasonably happy families contribute to buoyant communal morale, and add their own buzz and fizz to life in the cities.

As the cities have grown in size and stature, the bushman, the explorer, the pioneer, and the bushranger have all faded in the collective imagination. Anzac remains, and it has been reanimated. Annual rituals carry it, led by the Dawn Service, held in cities and towns, and articulated at a distance through admiration for national heroes, especially in sport. It may be significant that two of the country's most successful actors have played Achilles-like heroes in their major roles—Mel Gibson in *Braveheart* (1995), and Russell Crowe in *The Gladiator* (2000), with both films winning the Oscar for best picture of the year. In the same period, three of the most successful local films at the Australian box-office were unambiguously domestic—*Muriel's Wedding* (1994), *Babe* (1995), and *The Castle* (1997).

6

NATURE

Australia's epic stories have been set in the landscape. So too has its most influential and popular art, from the 1890s Heidelberg School to the 1950s wave of Nolan, Boyd, Tucker, and Drysdale.

Nature, whether on land or by sea, puts humans in their place. The sheer monumental vastness of oceans, cliffs, deserts, plains, forests, mountains, and the sky itself, together with the ferocious multiple onslaught of the elements, imposes a timeless and grand authority. A national consciousness grew early in the new settler society that this country cannot be conquered—in contradistinction from the progressive optimism that has characterised the United States, with its mythology of taming the West. The hero in the American Western is a commanding presence, riding nonchalantly through the landscape, even when that landscape is as grand as in Monument Valley (*The Searchers*). Horace Greeley's assumption of manifest destiny, reflected in his famous advice, 'Go West, young man, go West and grow up with the country', is inconceivable in Australia, where nature casts humans as nobodies.

Patrick White's Voss, the archetypal explorer of the Australian *inland*—driven by heroic will and a delusory fantasy of conquest—disappears into the unknown and dies. The best-known explorers, Burke and Wills, are remembered as a cautionary tale of folly. Even bushranger Ned Kelly fails—he projected as a kind of force of nature, with his quixotic armour riding through the bush. The powerful, Gothic horror of Barbara Baynton's bush stories and the *Mad Max* films depict nature as the menacing home to malevolent and even diabolical forces—ones that crush mere ordinary mortals. Similar imagery pervades, more recently, Tim Winton's novel *Dirt Music* (2001). The malevolence of nature has also been cast in romanticised colours, as in *Picnic at Hanging Rock*, novel and film, but it is no less menacing and dreadful for that.

In the nineteenth century, prospective settlers undertook months of perilous sea voyage only to find, in numerous cases, that their first sight of the new land was of crags and rocks, onto which storms dashed their ships. Danger was not met in the Atlantic Ocean sailing south down the long west coast of Africa, round the Cape of Good Hope, nor riding the gales and heaving tides of the Roaring Forties through the vast Southern Ocean, but within sight of the final destination on the Victorian coast. That coast, from Warrnambool to Cape Schanck, became littered with shipwrecks—638 ships are known to have foundered there.

Humans today are, in reality, threatened by bushfire, cyclone, drought, and flood—and not just in remote areas, for the fringes of Sydney, Canberra, Melbourne, and Adelaide are periodically ravaged by bushfire, as is Brisbane by flood. Those humans are menaced by snakes, crocodiles, sharks, and deadly spiders. The Queensland taipans are the most lethally poisonous snakes in the world. Steve Irwin entered national mythology as a Tarzan figure killed by a stingray (actually a minor killer in the Australian repertoire). During the Sydney Olympics, two fatal shark attacks let visitors who cared to notice know where they were—it was as if the land put on its own show. Even the birds are on average the most aggressive in the world—a magpie terrorised a Brisbane school for two weeks, pecking the faces of more than a hundred children.[129]

Farmers are afflicted by plagues of rabbits, mice, locusts, and cane toads; and by rampaging weeds like prickly pear. White ants can devour a wooden house, unbeknown to the occupants until the paint crinkles and the floorboards disintegrate under the feet—the one threat no insurance company will cover. In response to the multiple threats, the vast aridity, and the climatic extremes, the people huddle around the coastal rim, facing the sea and with their backs to the interior, repressing the 'dead heart' and the 'Never Never'. This demographic oddity is accentuated today, with the rural population contracting.

Farming in Australia engenders profound fatalism. It is subject, firstly, to the diabolical whims of nature, with most of the country exposed to chronically unreliable rainfall—seven years of drought may be followed by two seasons of flooding. It is subject, secondly, to international markets, which see the prices of wheat, wool, beef, lamb, cotton, and other primary products fluctuate wildly and unpredictably. It is subject, thirdly, to shifts in the value of the Australian dollar (for instance, more than doubling against the U.S. dollar between 2002 and 2011). Most farmers, in order to withstand harsh times, go into debt, and commonly very highly-geared debt, so that their fourth challenge is courting bank managers, and promising them the unpromisable. To survive in this domain, and with some remnants of sanity and balance intact, requires levels of philosophical detachment and a capacity for good-humoured resignation reminiscent of Greek tragedy. Love of the land and family pride may be fortified by a stubborn refusal to give in, and a quixotic defiance of omnipresent and malevolent fate. Don Watson has provided a harrowing personal account of his family running a small, dairy-farm in Gippsland.[130]

But nature also provides the *beach*. Balmy, euphoric, and revitalising, it is Australia's leading place of worship. The sensual pleasures of warm sand, cosseting sun, and the plunge into the bracing purity of the surf provide a kind of reawakening to a more alert and vibrant living; the profane human body and the tedium of the everyday are transformed—inspired and redeemed—as if by a benign supernatural power, itself sourced in nature and the cosmos. Tim Winton talks autobiographically, in relation to his novel *Breath* (2008), about stealing a morning to surf: 'Going down to the sea in anguish and turmoil and bewilderment, pubescent eruption, then coming home blissed out and happy. At one with the world.'[131]

Today, for urban Australians, the opening line from Dorothea Mackellar's popular nationalist poem, 'I love a sun-burnt country...' has its actual realisation in lazing on the sand by the water's edge. John Spooner, in a 1990s cartoon, imagined Adolf Hitler visiting an Australian beach to harangue the sun worshippers: they looked at the Nazi dictator in bemused disbelief, before lazily turning away. The cult of the beach spills over into the symbolic significance of Surf Lifesaving Clubs, and their exemplary volunteers, physically idealised as secular gods and goddesses. These voluntary associations are one of the few examples of sporting clubs not suffering from declining membership.

Matthew Arnold linked his famous 1867 lament over the retreat of the Sea of Faith to Dover Beach:

> *But now I only hear*
> *Its melancholy, long, withdrawing roar,*
> *Retreating, to the breath*
> *Of the night wind, down the vast edges drear*
> *And naked shingles of the world.*

Australian poet Chris Wallace-Crabbe, reflecting on the beach as our quintessential national experience, mocked: 'But fancy Matthew Arnold's beach having been just wet stones! Bugger that for a joke, I reckoned.'[132] Faith down under had risen in counter movement to Arnold's ebbing tide.

But even relaxing in idyllic reverie on the beach, lying in warm sand, lulled by the deep rhythms of the ocean swell, the sublime is ambivalent. The glistening turquoise water harbours deadly rips, poisonous jelly-fish, and killer sharks. And not all who go down to the sea, do so to relax. Winton's *Breath* centres on boys and men seeking ever more extreme and dangerous encounters with nature, and especially with the surf. It is if they, belonging to the nation's class of compulsive gamblers, are drawn, in intoxicated flirtation, towards a death embrace with the elements—the ultimate gamble.

The cities function as oases of fertility and climatic moderation on the edge, pressed in a narrow strip between the vast interior and the ocean. They provide genial habitats in which to live and to work. Their pleasantness and conviviality might be expected to induce a casual, even careless indolence—indeed, Ronald Conway argued as much in the 1970s.[133] But city culture has tended, in recent decades, as I have already argued, to press in the opposite direction, encouraging seriousness about life, an engagement with it, and the drive to take it on. This paradox at the core of the nation's character may have its roots in the ambivalences that emanate from the awesome power of nature that frames the Australian experience.

Patrick White, in his major novels—above all *Voss* (1957) and *Riders in the Chariot* (1961)—tried to plot a way along which the newcomers to this ancient continent might find their metaphysical bearings. Only time will tell how successful he was. White knew that the need to feel at home would only be answered in relation to the land.

The nation seems untroubled by anachronisms. It accepts the

fact that March flies come in January—if it were February, the naming might be passed off as a slip. It keeps the Queen of Britain as its constitutional head. Michael Leunig, in a February, 1998 newspaper cartoon, portrayed the Monarchy as a huge old Bentley blowing smoke, a tiny chauffeur propped behind the wheel, a tiny becrowned Queen alone in the backseat. Its caption read: 'Rust in chassis and panels; Limited spare parts; Steering heavy; Brakes—subtle to light; Excellent shock absorbers; Lots of character; Acceleration—gradual; Ash trays—beautiful.' The Republic was a minibus sardine-packed with gloomy people, massive bullbars in front, the President on the roof reclining expansively on a banana chair, belted down and with airbag protection. Leunig might have added bureaucrats lining the street, clapping.

A toleration of anachronism relates to a deeper political instinct. The Anglo tradition has been loath to codify procedures, preferring to rely on common sense and inherited civic customs to manage change. It moves in contradistinction to what might be called the rationalist canon, according to which optimism about human nature is combined with confidence about the capacity of human intelligence to understand complicated institutions, ones which have taken generations of accumulated wisdom to build. The rationalist canon assumes that major reforms scripted according to planned blueprints will not lead to serious unforeseen consequences—the belief in such reforms represents a type of excess. The Anglo tradition is at odds with the bureaucratic centralism native to France, Spain, Italy, and Germany.

Moreover, the rationalist impulse is towards a sort of order in which all contradictions are ironed out, and with them the red herrings and encumbrances which are to be found in the thick of lived life and its social muddle. I deliberately mix the metaphors, for culture is like that, when viewed from a dispassionate distance.

It drips with unaesthetic clutter. It is enough to drive purist social engineers mad.

Children, as David Tacey has observed, love dinosaurs.[134] The fact that dinosaurs are long dead, comprehensively extinct, somehow makes them more alive in the imagination. They are so unlike any creature inhabiting today's actual world, nightmare monsters yet fetching in their colossal clumsiness, an abomination to the orderly mind. This all suits them to the mythic domain, that in which culture, itself a type of living organism, belongs. Moreover, children who are enchanted by their dreams, their fantasies, do not have the slightest anxiety about identity.

We seem to have learnt, from the Aborigines as much as our own heritage, that in order to dwell at ease in this country, it is essential to possess the land in some spiritual sense—or rather to be possessed by it. That long and enigmatic process is surely well underway, although it is difficult to chart. One indicator is the place in our imagination occupied by the array of weird and unique animals that populate *Terra Australis*. To note just one positive—our coinage has for four decades now been graced by spirited, brilliant images of some of them.

Take the echidna, the spiny anteater well chosen as one of the animals to represent the nation at the Sydney Olympics. It totters along crashing clumsily through the bush—lucky that it only stalks ants—its gait part-waddle, part-roll, part-heave, its walk as if on its wrists with clawed forepaws flapping forward and backward-pointing hind feet awkwardly thrusting along. This lonely nomad somehow manages to cover kilometres a day, demolishing nest after nest, corkscrewing into them with its pencil snout. What is more, it has a ridiculous reproductive system, a mammal that lays a single egg out of its anus, somehow shifts it into a pouch where the hatchling sucks at milk pores. In any rational terms, the echidna should suffer crippling identity crisis.

Yet it is spectacular at survival, whether in mountain snow, desert, or thick bush. It is a notorious escape artist, known to break out of almost any type of box, to tunnel, to climb trees or two-metre cyclone fences. And strong—one was reported to have got free by moving a refrigerator across a kitchen.

Everything about this spiny anteater, now titled *tachyglossus*, meaning 'fast tongue', is anachronism, Australia's own living miniature dinosaur. Scientists once called it the 'living fossil'. Even the name is absurdly inappropriate, its Greek mythological ancestor, *echidna*, being a snake. And there is nothing fast about it, apart perhaps from its tongue. It is marvellous too that we know so little about it—as if it has flummoxed intrusive human attempts to document its ways of being.

There is something strangely reassuring out in the bush when one hears close by the snapping twigs and crushing leaves, the plodding movement of a creature low, heavy and slow. Perhaps it is something akin to having Tubby Taylor in charge, knowing that 'fast tongue' is near.

The echidna teaches a love of certain types of irrationality, and helps confirm a relaxed relationship to anachronisms. It is an order-loving, tidy bureaucrat's nightmare. And yet, as I have argued, Australian civic culture places strong emphasis on order.

There is no contradiction here. Stable politics, pleasant and efficient cities, hard-working citizens, and cheerful sociability represent the framing structure that the settlers have built by means of their own wit and industry. This structure is what has been within their own human powers, within their capacity for creating a world as they want it. Nature reminds them that much remains beyond their powers. Forces move that are far more powerful than anything those settlers may conjure up, forces that may strike with instant and cataclysmic effect. Within this humbling metaphysical context, why should the people trouble about anachronisms that do not impinge on practical living? More, such anachronisms, like the echidna, are a benign, even humorous reminder of those settlers' own feeble imaginations.

Treading a middle course, there is a major tradition in Australian life and culture that views the human relationship to the country as friendly. It follows the *I love a sun-burnt country* line. In Arthur Streeton's painting of *The Land of the Golden Fleece* (1926), a flock of sheep, a few cattle, a stockman on horseback, and a man chopping wood—no more distinctive than dry grass and eucalypt—all blend harmoniously into a parched landscape. There is a spare beauty here, the Grampians in the background, resonant with the bluish transcendent glow of some beyond. Diminishing the humans and their enterprises, a grander stillness pervades the land. Streeton wrote to his friend, painter Tom Roberts:

> *I fancy large canvases all glowing and moving in the happy light and others bright decorative and chalky and expressive of the hot trying winds and the slow immense summer. It is IMMENSE, and the droughts and cracks in the earth and creeks all baked mud.*[135]

If the gods are present, though, their domain does not permit explicit human tracery. The mountain in *The Land of the Golden Fleece* is not Mt Sinai—no God will appear to present the stone tablets of the Law to the people. And as the nation's stories suggest, the country will rebuff those who rise above themselves. Would-be prophets and leaders who try to usurp the primacy of the place will fail in it.

The instruction and the warning are not just against excess

and superfluity. The men in the Streeton scene are, like the great majority who populate the land—they in their cities—fringe dwellers. Patrick White, in his masterpiece, *Riders in the Chariot*, embraces this reality as nothing but well and fair. The sanest of his chosen ones, Mrs Godbold, lives in a dilapidated shed with her many children. It is there, as, once upon a time in a Bethlehem cattle shed, that the fundamental event takes place. Mrs Godbold, too, represents White's projection of women as being more likely to find themselves at home, in uncomplaining acceptance of the hardships of life.

At issue are *proper-ties*. Property is the profane starting point. Just what do we possess? Are we merely occupying space? European Australians are becoming more self-conscious about the possibility that there could be a spirit to the land. It may project its own aura. It may even preside. They are intrigued by the Aboriginal mode of engagement. As different, even alien, as the way of the original inhabitants may be, perhaps it does hold some secret. Above all, there is the stress that proper ties oblige those who pitch camp to become faithful servants of place—they belong to it, rather than any bit of it belonging to them. As an echo, Australian property law is unlike its American equivalent in not granting landowners rights to the minerals lying beneath their soil.

The furthest the fringe dwellers usually go in practice are Romantic, tamed encounters with the Bush—retreating to live in Pearl Bays by the sea, surfing in life-saver protected strips between ocean-beach flags, cultivating native gardens, and adventuring out in caravan tours round the coastal rim, as retired couples commonly do, in timid and amateurish simulation of the Voss journey of exploration. They do not want to be heroes.

The suburban home stands partly as fenced-in defence against infinitude of landscape, the boundlessness reverberating through laconic sprawling cities. Occupation remains a troubled category, and will continue so until the newcomers take in the Aboriginal lesson about how to dwell in order to belong. That lesson is about being.

And yet, dwelling on the fringe, Australians live closer to their nature than most European or American counterparts, closer to the elements. Whether in teeming rain, howling gale, scorching heat, or pounding surf there is something uplifting and invigorating in the proximity, subjected to the power, humbled. Film director Peter Weir gives powerful evocation to the Australian version of Romantic pantheism. In *Picnic at Hanging Rock* (1975), it is an outcrop of rock that marshals the sacred force to spirit teenage girls away; in *The Last Wave* (1977), the tactile presence of torrential water overwhelms bewildered Sydney city-dwellers, tapping into Aboriginal dreaming.

Australians cherish being 'outdoors'. Their ideal homes connect large living rooms—lounge, kitchen, and dining—with direct access to courtyard or backyard. That access itself is visually open, with separation by means of plate-glass doors, via ample verandas with their own barbeque facilities, dining tables, and lounge chairs. Garden and sky become integrated into domestic space. This vernacular style includes interest in climate, and being tuned in to changes in the weather. Ideally, there are landscape views from the main veranda, of distant mountains, wild bush, or of water—one of the appeals of Sydney Harbour is that its scores of inlets and coves provide views for tens of thousands of houses. And, the utopia that is beach is not just one of the mind, for easy access means that all city-dwellers can experience it at will, as most do. The experience of stronger light and brighter colours, compared to Europe, encourages optimism and cheerfulness.

On a grander scale, the nation's preeminent building in architectural terms, the Sydney Opera House, is set on its own promontory, with water on three sides, and its fourth facing the city. It is set in nature, and as such is quite unlike Europe's most prominent buildings, with the partial exception of the Parthenon. The country's second most distinguished building, the Canberra War Memorial, is set on the side of a hill, framed by eucalypt forest, overlooking the city. In look, it belongs to the bush.

Patrick White reads the country as receptive to wayward vision. It is there in a film hit of the 1990s—*The Castle*. Set in another shed, in another fringe suburb, the scene is Melbourne wasteland—at least as judged by prevailing standards of charm, taste, and comfort. Yet, to the father's eye it is his little corner of paradise. The love and energy with which he puts his vision of home into practice nurtures a very happy family. The film flirts with the quixotic ludicrousness of this man, as did Roy and HGs *Dream* with sport stars, and can do so because of that intangible Australian security of being which is not prickly about prestige and dignity. Such security is antipode to the 'cultural cringe' felt by sections of the intelligentsia—for whom uprootedness seems to be a life condition. There are traces in *The Castle* of many a suburban backyard—a blessed little corner. Just ask the children who grew up in them!

Special warmth has grown for kangaroo, wallaby, koala, wombat, platypus, and echidna. While they represent a singularly engaging and charming assembly, and an arrestingly odd one in the context of the world's wild animals, the love of them is more than that of the cuddly-toy sort. The marsupials set a tone, in their way of being. In part, it is their lack of aggression—except when cornered. There is the quiet way they go about negotiating their habitat—the solitary wallaby in the bush stopping to cock an ear and look, before gracefully loping away. It shares an affinity with the way the people respond to bureaucratic controls. Calm resistance, except when cornered, has met the Australia Card, Byzantine new tax systems, and grand attempts to tidy up the Constitution.

The Muddle-headed Wombat is one of Australia's finest and best-loved children's books. Written by Ruth Park, its first appearance was as a 1950s ABC radio serial. Park's wombat is good-natured and warm-hearted, but also an amusing anachronism, being fat with short legs, clumsy, and mangling his words in a charmingly muddle-headed way. Most endearing is his ease of being, a quiet self-possessed composure that accompanies him as he goes about his chosen business, whatever it might be, from eating snails to playing pirates, from rescuing children lost in the dark to sitting on his friends.

The kookaburra reminds humans, prone to taking themselves seriously, that they are easy to laugh at. Don't we recognise its cadences in the raucous vulgar zest of Barry Humphries' most brilliant satiric creation—the Falstaffian cultural ambassador, Sir Les Patterson? Then there was the wombat star of the Sydney Games. And how many Australians who travel overseas feel reassured when they first spot the kangaroo, indicating that a Qantas plane has arrived—something familiar and trusted? The totemism of Aboriginal tribal culture seems to be colonising the colonisers.

We have stumbled upon a paradox. The temperament of the people is cheerful, practical, amiable, modest, and sceptical. It is reflected in the civic culture, in the Romantic Streeton-style vision of man and woman set in landscape, and in a hoped-for affinity with the wombat and the other genial native creatures. Yet, flitting in the background, like dark spirits in a midsummer night's dream, are warning signs, portents, and cautionary episodes. The wider, and seemingly encompassing context, is that of sublime threat. The magpie is virtually unique among world birds in voicing both beautiful songs and harsh attack calls.[136]

A man was found mysteriously dead on his front veranda, on the fringes of Melbourne in the 1990s. Five snakebites were observed on his arms and legs. A dead tiger snake lay next to him, with two human bites taken out of its body. It seems that the man had staggered home drunk the night before, lurched up steps onto the veranda, and stood on the snake in the dark. The snake bit him, so he retaliated by grabbing it, and in a drunken fury wrestling it to the death—of both of them. The most prominent national news story of the 1970s was that of a mother, Lindy Chamberlain, charged with killing her baby at a camping ground at Uluru in Central Australia—it turned out that a dingo had taken the infant. Steve Irwin, known as 'the crocodile hunter', became an international television celebrity because of dare-devil, close encounters with Australia's killer creatures, only to be struck a hundred times by the tail of a 2-metre-wide sting-ray he was filming, before being lethally pierced through the heart by the tail-spine.

Voss found his own real-life incarnation on 17 December, 1967. Australian Prime Minister Harold Holt walked into the surf at Cheviot Bay, Portsea, and swam out between rocks towards a deep rock pool, which he always enjoyed. He found himself in a vicious undertow, swam with it, only to be ripped out to sea, never to be seen again. A friend who watched helplessly from the shore later said, 'He was like a leaf being taken out. It was so quick and so final.' All the surf lifesavers to search that afternoon did so in fear: the sea was ferocious, with five-metre waves breaking over the reef. Divers searching for the Prime Minister had to be recalled repeatedly, because of the seas, the cloudbursts, and the gales.

Mr Holt was no amateur swimmer, but a spear-fisherman of long experience. He knew and loved the Portsea coast in Victoria intimately. The dangers of going swimming that afternoon would have been starkly obvious to him—swimming in a notoriously dangerous stretch of water, one that had wrecked dozens of ships in the nineteenth century. Harold Holt had just arrived from Canberra, where he was struggling with political difficulties, and he presumably felt the need to take the risk, to plunge into the surf to cleanse himself of worldly pollutants. Head of a nation of gamblers, he took the ultimate throw of the dice. The last sight of him was of his silver hair, as he appeared to be swimming strongly with the current.

American Presidents are surrounded by scores of bodyguards and phalanxes of security agents, for the threat to them is from humans, in the form of assassination. Harold Holt signals a different civic context, one in which Prime Ministers are still able to mingle freely in crowds. To be accompanied to Cheviot Beach by bodyguards would have been culturally ludicrous, and deeply embarrassing to the Prime Minister. Moreover, they would have been useless, when confronted by a deadly rip.

Portents is what we have here, flashes of fire occasionally rising from beneath the tranquil surface of everyday life. As in *The Iliad*, months may pass into years for the hero, ordinarily spent with him lounging on the fringe of the field of battle, at leisure, entertaining himself and his companions with feasting, chat, and playing the lyre and singing. In Australia, everyday life tends to pass in an easy, amiable, and comfortable manner. Then, on an instant, the Greek hero's composure is shattered, when his bosom friend is killed in battle, and timeless darkness settles over his world. The most lethal Australian bushfires have come to be known as 'Black Friday, 1939', 'Ash Wednesday, 1983', and 'Black Saturday, 2009'.

Australian nature teaches reverence for a grander scheme than the mortal human. It places human endeavour in perspective. It provides a potentially all-encompassing context for life, marrying awesome beauty with powerful threat—a context that can be, at once, alerting and invigorating. It teaches modesty, balance, and a kind of realist fatalism about the ineffectuality of human will in relation to the major turning points in a life. It dampens any naive optimism about individual or social progress. The nation's sceptical habit of mind may have its inspiration here.

7
THREATS

The argument of this book has worked with the country's strengths. I want, in this chapter, to turn to weaknesses, and potential threats to the economic prosperity and high civic morale that I have been charting. I shall suggest that there are three such weaknesses and threats.

a. Civic Leadership.

Paul Kelly concluded, in his definitive political history of the Keating-Howard years, that the country had benefited from very able political leadership.[137] This had been accompanied by the high competence of senior public officials, and notably of Ian Macfarlane, Governor of the Reserve Bank.[138] Kelly, in effect, gives support to the general thesis put later by Ian McLean in *Why Australia Prospered*. Likewise, the case-study of Melbourne's development over the last quarter century has shown the vital role played by civic leadership. That story would have been very different without visionary planning and execution at both the City Council and State Government levels.

The characterisation of Australia as the 'lucky country' has been as false as it is malign. Horne's phrase stuck, partly because of lack of alternatives. Geoffrey Blainey, in his histories of Australian mining, has shown how much success has depended on inspiration, initiative, and resourcefulness, followed by gruelling and unremitting work, usually in harsh environments.

Gold nuggets did not fall out of the sky; nor did iron ore, nickel, diamonds, and alumina. Equally, we know the response from those who farm if we were to quote Horne at them. We would be instructed that droughts, bushfires, floods, frosts, rabbits, dingoes, locusts, mouse plagues, not to mention fickle world commodity prices, are truly, one and all, signs of luck.

Nor were the Sydney Olympics merely the product of fortune—given what they represent in terms of a society's capacity for large-scale organisation, starting with well-designed and efficient infrastructure. Nor was the Bradman phenomenon. Indeed, the parameters for the right way of going about human business in this country were put in one of the Don's innings, as described by Neville Cardus: 'It was never uninteresting; he simply abstained from vanity and rhetoric.' Bean might have written the same, in graver tones, of the Diggers. *Never uninteresting—abstaining from vanity and rhetoric* could serve as the nation's motto. That Bradman performance was based on a boyhood spent in relentless practice, and three gifts—lightening reflexes, formidable intelligence, and superhuman powers of concentration.

But Bradmans are rare. There have been periods of poor leadership, and missed opportunities. For nine years between 2007 and 2017, the country was cursed by being led by three poor Prime Ministers in a row, and likely four. The question arose of how long it could withstand weak government without medium-term damage to its institutions.

Among a string of planning debacles during the Rudd-Gillard Labor years, the move to implement a National Broadband Network was arguably the most expensive folly. Launched without any cost-benefit analysis, its final bill could have risen to around $80b, sucking public money out of far more worthy infrastructure building. Private enterprise would have provided an equivalent service to the cities, without any cost to Government, leaving Canberra to take responsibility for remote and regional Australia, as has always been necessary. As symbol of government imposed inefficiency, the NBN could only work by legislating itself as a monopoly, and by buying off its one plausible competitor, Telstra. Here was regression to a long-discredited socialist way of centralist thinking. By the time Labor lost office in 2013, the NBN Corporation was virtually paralysed by delays, mega-cost overruns, and by very low take-up of its service in the few areas in which it had been laid.

Another serious area of mismanagement over the last decade or so has been in energy policy. By 2017, electricity and gas supply were under threat, with both commercial and domestic users afflicted by rapidly increasing costs. Blackouts in South Australia were predicted to be merely harbingers of what would hit the larger Eastern States. For a country that has abundant supplies of gas and coal—not to mention uranium, sun, and wind—the failure to replace ageing energy infrastructure, and manage a slow shift to alternative renewable forms of energy, represents planning incompetence of the first order—and at both Commonwealth and State levels. In 2004, Australia had the cheapest energy costs in the OECD; thirteen years later it had slid well down the list. A major competitive advantage for Australian business had been squandered.

The Labor years were followed by a clumsy and largely ineffectual Liberal Abbott Government, and then a dithering Turnbull successor. Weakness in the leadership of the two main parties has facilitated the rise of independents and minor parties, notably in the Senate, making government decisions subject to complex negotiation, and far more difficult to implement. This was compounded in the July 2016 election, with a close result leading to an even more tangled Senate, and even greater challenges to governability. Above all, any future Federal government will need the will and the aptitude to overcome interest groups, obstructionist political parties, and an increasingly sceptical public, in order to cut its own expenditure and raise taxation—thereby repairing the budget.

The paralysis that has bedevilled many European governments in relation to long-term policy could be manifesting itself in Australia, with changes to the functioning of the Federal parliament that may be more structural than just the result of short-term electoral ups-and-downs. If so, the country will become less able to adapt to changing conditions, both international and internal; it will become less well governed in the ways outlined by Ian McLean in *Why Australia Prospered*.

Since Federation, it is as if Australian settlement has remained—with the partial exception of the building of Canberra—fixated in nineteenth-century geography. It is still stuck with the doomed explorers Burke and Wills at Cooper's Creek, unable to bridge the continent. Governments from both sides missed a golden opportunity in the last thirty years of developing Darwin into a new Singapore or Hong Kong. They failed for want of the great vision that had backed large-scale post-war immigration.

Imagine Darwin as the nation's third major city! The ramifications are profound. It would function as an Asian money, securities, and trade centre anchored by the stability of Australian democracy and its independent, corruption-free, legal and financial institutions. Australia has the huge comparative advantage over other OECD countries of being close to the Asian market-place, an advantage that will only grow with time. Such a developed Darwin, located on the doorstep of Southeast Asia, would facilitate the inevitable future ties between this country and those to the north. Its own more Asian multicultural cast would help adapt a predominantly Anglo-European society to its shifting geo-political location. The main competitor in the region, Hong Kong, has a questionable medium-term future, given likely continuing encroachment on its freedoms by a corrupt, totalitarian government in Beijing.

Specific developments would automatically follow—for instance, a fast train link to the south. The vast area of the Kimberley's—fertile and water-rich—could be developed from Darwin. The entire balance and orientation of the nation would change. The current centre of social and wealth mass in the southeast corner would swing up and towards the middle. A greater harmony might follow between the geographical stretch of this vast continent and its human imaginings. National development on this scale, of both time and scope, depends on active, interventionist planning and direction from Canberra.

The leading general challenge today is planning to build infrastructure, and implementing those plans. This is well-known and uncontroversial. The major cities will suffocate with projected population increases, unless they are better articulated by roads, rail, and linked facilities (schools, infant welfare centres, parks, playgrounds, and shopping hubs). The solution lies with State Governments, with support from Canberra, and support from their own electorates willing to focus on the longer-term and accept the cost and disruption that inevitably accompanies large-scale development. On this front, recent governments do not compare well with their Victorian-era predecessors.

Brisbane provides an encouraging example of visionary development over the last quarter-century. Wayne Goss, Premier from 1989, and Arts Minister, prepared much of the way. Jim Soorley, elected Mayor of Brisbane in 1992, drove the development of better urban infrastructure. Then, the Beattie Government (1998-2007) had two strikingly successful 'Smart State' initiatives.[139] One was the $300m development of a thriving arts precinct on the south bank of the Brisbane River. The Gallery of Modern Art opened in 2006, and, with the Art Gallery of Queensland, it has managed to increase attendance fourfold, and outperform the National Gallery of Victoria. A fine new State Library of Queensland opened in 2008, and in the same period the Brisbane Festival expanded.

The South Bank of the river has been transformed into a vital communal centre of activity and leisure. Griffith University, from the 1990s, moved its cultural faculties onto the South Bank, populating the area with staff and students. The excellent quarterly cultural magazine *Griffith Review* was launched in 2003. The second Smart State achievement has been major support for universities and research institutes, with the help of private philanthropy, resulting in the increased standing of the University of Queensland, and the development of thriving biotechnology research.

b. Bureaucracy.

'The characteristic talent of Australians is for bureaucracy', wrote A. F. Davies in 1958.[140] The judgment was plausible during the golden years of the Commonwealth Public Service in the 1950s and 1960s. Departments were headed by the famous 'Menzies' midgets', or 'seven dwarfs', men who while short in height were prodigiously able and had benefited from a broad life-experience, coming from diverse backgrounds framed by economic depression and World War.[141] Davies' judgment about Australia's talent for bureaucracy has become less convincing with time.

Kenneth Hopper and William Hopper have analysed the decline of the American corporation since 1970, in their book *The Puritan*

Gift (2007).¹⁴² Their examples include General Motors, General Electric, and NASA. The Hoppers single out four ruinous factors: top-down management replacing bottom-up innovation; the focus shifting from the quality of product to finance, as accountants replace engineers in senior management roles; the increasing emphasis on management as a science, dependent on statistics; and the intrusion of the culture of the MBA, started at Harvard in 1908 (degrees that taught people how to take over companies, but not how to run them).

In Australia, similar symptoms have emerged in public and private sector bureaucracies. The universities are a case in point. Thirty years ago they were institutions that appointed academics and then left them pretty much alone, to publish and teach what they liked (the key to a fine academy, then as now, is judgment in making appointments). A creative industry needs minimal bureaucracy. According to Peter Murphy, modern universities have spent 20 cents in the dollar on administration for most of their history; this had risen to 40c by 1931, 50c by 1970—it is now 70c.¹⁴³ 55% of university staff are now non-academic. In most Australian universities, senior management neutered the influence of professors twenty years ago.

In my own institution, 34% of the total budget goes to central administration. One consequence is a shift to top-down management, exemplified in abstract new teaching models designed by 'teaching and learning' administrators being imposed on experienced academics who have refined their teaching practices over many years. The typical restructure leads to fewer hands-on administrative staff, where they are needed at the interface between students and lecturers, and more at higher levels, detached from the practical work of the institution.

In the new university, furthermore, there are dwindling funds to employ tutors, so students suffer from larger class sizes and less direct contact with teachers. In my own department in 2013, the academic staff was taxed 70% by the University (only 30% of what they earned from the fees of the students they taught went on their salaries).

Universities are being flooded by a new wave of pseudo-rationality. 'Metrics' is one of the buzzwords. Everything must be made measurable. Another buzzword is 'outcomes'. Outcomes must be quantified. To some degree this is necessary: students are assessed—by essay, exam, or whatever—and they are ranked, and given qualifications. But in the new order a gigantic Benthamite calculus is being developed, to subject more and more elements in the path of education to measurement, with a view to maximising the end numbers.

Australian has developed a malign tertiary education model, a bureaucratic centralist one more suited to the Spanish tradition. The universities are run from Canberra, where central command has been mainly responsible for the transformation in university culture over the last thirty years, both through general example and specific interference. The Federal bureaucracy has steadily increased its monitoring requirements—cracking the whip in terms of the number of reports on performance required from its mendicants, who depend on it for funding (supplying 56% of total university funding in 2011, if a declining percentage).

In comparative international terms, Australia has much better quality schools than it does universities (with none close to being ranked in the top twenty in the world, although sections within them, such as Melbourne University Law, do rank very highly). This is largely a result of the competition that has flowed from a multi-dimensional system of public and private schooling. The success of the Australian Institute of Sport proves that the country can build first-class teaching bodies if it puts its mind to it. The multi-dimensional schooling system has parallels with the American university model, which in itself has produced scores of first-rank institutions, both private and public. The Australian tertiary model had been three-tier until the Hawke Government, in 1992, reclassified Colleges of Advanced Education as universities—arguably that Government's worst decision during a decade in power (the third tier, TAFEs, provide training in technical skills). The imposed homogeneity inevitably told against quality.

Centralised bureaucracy has a tendency to cultivate mediocrity. For instance, the Australian Research Council administers funding for research. Academics, in order to receive grants for research, are subjected to an application process of byzantine complexity and length, which in reality serves as an endurance test in bureaucratic game-playing, and bears little relationship to the potential quality of research, certainly in the humanities. Typically, in the new order, research output is assessed in terms of metrics: points published per staff member per year, with, for instance, five points for a book, irrespective of its quality. Darwin's *The Origin of Species* would be ranked equally with a treatise on basket-weaving in Bendigo. To amend one of the Hoppers' factors of ruin, Australia's universities are switching attention from quality of product to conformity to bureaucratic process.

Australia's future prosperity will largely depend on creative and knowledge industries, which in their turn depend on the quality of primary, secondary, and tertiary education. The standard of universities becomes ever more important to the national interest. I have a friend engaged in biotechnology start-up companies, who refuses to employ chemists trained in Australian universities—on the grounds that their competency compares unfavourably with that of overseas graduates. If 'location, location, location' is the mantra of real-estate agents, then that of the universities, as of all creative organisations, should be 'excellence, excellence, excellence'.

Schools are under threat from the same tendency to replace pedagogy with bureaucratic process. An eminent private school in Melbourne now assesses the innate ability of each student then tests every fortnight whether, in each particular class, the teacher is managing to bring students above their expected level, or falling short. Parents are invited to participate in this scheme, harassing any poor teacher for whom the number dips beneath the ascribed norm. Teaching is turned into routinised accountancy, with any inspiration, flair, or spirit of adventure squeezed out—as both too risky, and requiring too much energy, very little of which a teacher has left after the relentless regimen of assessment and reporting, all conducted under the watchful eye of both school management and parents.

Some government schools are heading down the same path, with gifted vocational teachers leaving the profession in despair. Over the last decade, furthermore, the quality of students drawn into teacher training, as measured by academic results, has been in steady and marked decline.

On a more positive note, there is the recent entrepreneurship of some universities in contributing to civic vitality, as they build faculties in their respective CBDs. I have earlier noted the innovative role played by Griffith in Brisbane, the University of South Australia in Adelaide, and RMIT in Melbourne.

Bureaucracy is not capable of making substantive judgments. It does not innovate; it reacts and checks. Its expertise is in administering the given, and in reviewing due process and efficiency. In the sphere of culture its limitations are severe. I chaired a Panel reviewing the National Museum of Australia for the Commonwealth Government in 2003. The Review Panel's main finding was that the Museum was weak at presenting engaging displays of key moments in the nation's past; weak at vivid narrative. One problem was the appointment of Museum Directors whose background was in administration. If, say, specific displays had been contracted out to tested film directors, like Peter Weir and George Miller, to stage them cinematographically, there would be a much better chance of the public's inspired immersion in Australian history. The Report had the further challenge of resisting pressure from some of the senior public servants servicing it, pressure to tone down its prose, and render it in more abstract and evasive, official jargon.[144]

Bureaucracy becomes inbred, without external reality checks such as the discipline under which corporations have to perform—that of making a profit. There seems to be an inner law of bureaucratic development over time, of increasingly making rules for their own senseless sake, and inventing processes that are purely self-referential. The English television satire *Yes Minister* supplied the ultimate logic: one of the nation's top civil servants rhapsodised that the perfect hospital was one in which there were no patients. A current university joke is that management is working towards an ideal institution in which there are no academics.

To give a tragic example, bushfires that ravaged Victoria in February 2009, killing two hundred people, were followed by a Royal Commission. The Commission heard numerous reports of emergency-service and fire-fighting officers who were so overwhelmed by the bureaucratic order they were meant to be administering that they neglected to do the one obvious and crucial thing: warn people in danger that fire was approaching. Lost in their processes, they forgot to yell out: 'Fire!'

In recent years, the Commonwealth Public Service has shown signs of decreasing capability. Its most powerful department, the Treasury, has tarnished its professional image with a decade of flagrantly inaccurate economic forecasts. Earlier generations of more worldly officials may have been less enamoured of mathematical modelling. And a former Head, Ken Henry, damaged the Treasury's reputation for political independence by entering public debate, on environmental and other issues.[145] The Rudd Government responded to the Global Financial Crisis of 2008 with a series of Keynesian stimulatory measures, including a scheme to provide free ceiling insulation for homes. What became known as the 'Pink Batts scandal', with rushed and shoddy installations resulting in four deaths, was largely blamed on the bureaucratic incompetence of the Department administering the scheme.

Bureaucratic centralism is alien to the Anglo political model—the Anglo world has limited talent for it. Countries should stick to the strengths of their cultural traditions—those, for instance, with a strong social democratic past like Germany and Sweden have developed an institutional intelligence suited to their own model. Which is not to deny that there is a universal civic law decreeing the need to balance prudent regulation and promiscuous red-tape. A society needs building codes that restrict slipshod foundations, dodgy wiring, and poor insulation; but not a proliferation of permits that delay construction, and serve to escalate costs. Central bureaucracy, of its nature, wildly reproduces itself, unless periodically checked and renewed—with purges, culling, and reforming.

Australia is not alone in suffering from the cancerous creep of bureaucracy. And the problem is not new. It was diagnosed in 1915 by German socialist, Robert Michels, in his classic study *Political Parties*. Central to the logic of modernisation is an irresistible drive to make life more rational, more orderly, better documented, and progressively less subject to the risky and the unpredictable. Good planning, clear process, and standardised rules are accorded high value; and their implementation inevitably requires bureaucracy. In part, this is necessary, and to the good—as long as the work of the office is geared to an external goal, such as making a profit, educating a student, or providing medical care. Administrators are servants of their organisation. But beyond the limits of their vocational ethic—one stipulating modest service—a line is crossed, and a new beast emerges, that of rampaging, unbridled administration, followed by a slide into institutional paralysis. The creeping spread of the bureaucratic disease can be observed today not just in universities, schools, and government; but also in hospitals, nursing homes, emergency services, and local councils; and across the wide spectrum of medium and large business, including the larger sporting codes. Jerry Pournelle has amplified Robert Michels, coining the term 'the iron law of bureaucracy':

> *In any bureaucratic organization there will be two kinds of people: those who work to further the actual goals of the organization, and those who work for the organization itself. Examples in education would be teachers who work and sacrifice to teach children, vs. union representatives who work to protect any teacher including the most incompetent. The Iron Law states that in all cases, the second type of person will always gain control of the organization, and will always write the rules under which the organization functions.*[146]

Joseph Schumpeter went so far in 1942, in his classic *Capitalism, Socialism and Democracy*, to predict the downfall of capitalism, due to the bureaucratisation of large corporations squeezing out entrepreneurial drive, as committees replaced individuals.[147]

c. Decline of the Parent Culture.

The third threat to Australian prosperity and morale is more intangible. It operates at the deeper cultural level. A country's strength depends on its cultural gene pool. The framing consciousness and mythic sense draws upon three levels of tradition. Firstly, there is the long stretch of Western culture starting with the ancient Greeks and including the Jesus narratives. Secondly, there is the Anglo background of English legends, a literature anchored by Shakespeare and the King James Bible, the common law and parliament, and common-sense democratic customs, which include the honouring of contracts and covenants, and a presiding belief in individual freedom. Thirdly, there is the local Australian development discussed above in Chapters 4, 5, and 6.

Europe is in decline, as reflected since 2008 in a paralysed European Union that does not respect the rule of law; with many of its nations struggling to service towering levels of public debt; with stagnant economies; and with a refugee flood wrecking the EU principle of the free movement of peoples within its borders. This has been accompanied by a lack of political will to tackle the crisis of governance, an increasingly anti-political mood and polarisation of opinion in electorates, and the rise of populist and extremist leaders and parties. The British decision in 2016 to exit the EU can only serve to accelerate continental decline, whatever its consequences for Britain itself.

What will be the psychological impact on offspring societies as they lose respect for a waning parent? Will some kind of national Oedipal crisis emerge, or the opposite, a more self-assured independence?

Little problem may be anticipated at the highest level of tradition, that of Western culture in the fullness of its length and breadth. For over two thousand years, Greece as an actual country and society has manifested few of the hallmark qualities of its golden fifth-century BC ancestry, and especially in Athens. Yet, the classical Greek tradition has lived on in works of literature, philosophy, art, science, and architecture. As George Steiner has written of Jewish culture: its homeland is in the text, or in the word, not in a geographical place.[148] When Rome, Florence, and Paris have become like Delphi, Olympia, and the Athenian Acropolis—to be encountered as museums flavoured with a bit of local ambience—the Australian visitor won't notice much difference. The great texts written in literature, philosophy, art, music, and building, once produced by these centres of civilisation, will live on.

At the middle level of tradition, that of the Anglo-sphere, there could be more of a challenge. But, if Britain is to decline in parallel with much of Continental Europe, I doubt there will be significant impact in the offspring settler societies. By the beginning of the twenty-first century, England had completely lost its 'mother country' aura in Australia. The emotional tissues of attachment that had been vital up until 1942, and had continued to bind until the 1960s, had long withered. While the place of the Monarchy in the Constitution remains, it does so as a benign anachronism, which will likely stay put until it causes too much cultural strain. The central cluster of Australian legal, political, and administrative institutions are all thoroughly independent, and self-sustaining. Anglo loyalty and dependency, as much as it exists, has largely switched to the United States.

The U.S. that counts globally is Harvard and Yale, HBO and Hollywood, and Apple and Google. America remains the most creative society on earth, and by a vast margin. Consequently, whatever its current economic woes, it will likely recover. Mind, the challenge is immense, with low social mobility, no increase in the median wage in real terms in four decades, interest payments on federal government debt predicted to rise to 20% of tax revenues by 2020, and an electoral mood hostile to professional political elites, and susceptible to the appeal of populist, dilettante demagogues.[149]

For Australia, in particular, America's military pre-eminence is as important as its cultural creativity. As a fellow Anglo nation, middle-sized and of modest military capacity, situated alone on the fringe of Asia, it will continue to cling to the United States, in a rather lop-sided alliance, as long as the latter remains a world power.

The geo-political sands are shifting in the twenty-first century, with seeming inexorability. The Asia-Pacific region is emerging as the new hub of global economic and social dynamism. This raises new challenges (and opportunities) for Australia. What if China were to become a world power; if the Chinese language were to encroach on English as the world language; and if Singapore, Hong Kong, and Shanghai were to become the dominant cities in the Asia-Pacific region?

Let me put this hypothetical future into some perspective. Many are called and few are chosen in terms of the rise to world power—take note of what has happened to Japan since 1990, when there was near-consensus among experts that Japan would emerge as the next mega-power. And, the traditional world of empires is past, largely because wealth no longer depends on land. Above all, modernisation is an historical juggernaut that, so far, has carried everything in its path, seducing the societies that it encounters into conforming to its own ways. Today China, like Singapore and Hong Kong, is slavishly copying the West. The inner drive behind economic success seems to impel developing societies to become like us. The more powerful they become, the more Western they appear, in the way they look, they think, and they act.

At the same time, it is a sobering fact that the West has declined once before. Although the barbarians who successfully conquered Italy in the fifth-century AD proceeded to mimic Roman customs and practices—seemingly keeping the culture alive—the ensuing continuity led into the Dark Ages. The Roman Empire did not revive.

I have already speculated on the spin-off effect of Anglo-sphere confidence on Australia. Since Wellington's victory over Napoleon at the Battle of Waterloo in 1815, the globe has experienced two centuries of Anglo supremacy. In this period, the Anglo nations have become used to fighting wars and winning all of the major ones. Economic power has generated world power. It is telling that even though Britain is in the process of leaving the European Union, English will almost certainly remain the working language of that body.

The capitalist economy and parliamentary democracy, the two institutional creations that drive the modern world, were both intricate creations out of the culture of the people—its history, traditions, and institution-building capacities. We should never underestimate the enduring potency of *genesis*—its legacy. There may be a confidence deriving from a sort of instinctual knowledge that we as a people are moving and acting in a world that we know well, for we created it.

Important here is the language. This is the most difficult territory in which to find plausible tissues of connection. English, on the surface, displays a playful anarchic mayhem and freedom of structure that hides an implicit order of extraordinary complexity, an order which is, at best, crudely codified—and makes the language a nightmare for foreigners to learn to use well. We may discern some affinity with a legal culture hostile to codification, and inclined to the cumbersome and messy process of trial by jury; and a political tradition steeped in precedent, compromise, and common sense, one which vests authority in the basic wisdom of the common man and woman. The language and its peculiar ways may have helped to shape and steer the civic culture.

Also, the cadences of Shakespeare resound through the centuries; they were there to be heard, for instance, in the speeches of Winston Churchill. This, I suspect, is more than rhetoric, and flows into a way of thinking about the world, about politics, and into a conception of valour as a core part of national identity.

The Anglo-sphere remains, as always, dependent on the wider High Culture of the West. There is, to choose a notable example, the place in English of the first great foundational work—Homer's *Iliad*. George Steiner has noted the large number of translations into English since the Second World War—high in quality, and popular in demand—something unmatched in German or French.[150] A key aspect of cultural dynamism is maintaining a living relationship to the recurring motifs that shape understandings of the human condition. As already noted, the *Iliad* is of formative significance to Australia's own creation myth: it set the archetype for the warrior hero—the character, its ethos, and its obligations.

All in all, Australia has drawn heavily on a generalised Anglo-sphere confidence. The consequences will be potentially cataclysmic if the dominant nations within that tradition—firstly Britain, then the United States—do go into successive decline. However, the large-scale Asian immigration into Australia over the last two decades—principally Chinese and Indian—will act as a huge positive in terms of the future, and may help the development of of a hybrid Anglo-Asian culture, with analogies to Singapore and Hong Kong, but with the Anglo-Australian component more pronounced than in those two Asian cities.

But, to speculate further here would be fruitless. Prophecy is a calling for fools and madmen. In reflecting on the decline of Europe, and the possible impact of that decline on Australia, the task has merely been the sober one of locating parameters for what is likely to guide the future.

8

CONCLUSION

We inhabit the present, ideally responding as best we can to unforseen challenges and threats, exploiting opportunities as they come along, all the time striving to utilise our strengths, and negotiate around our weaknesses. Australia currently faces the future from a position of confidence, given a quarter century of sustained expansion and extraordinary prosperity. A period of economic slowdown will most likely be short-lived—unless international conditions and local responses to them take an extraordinary turn.

This book opened with Australia's exceptional economic performance. The performance is unique in the developed world, a fact that often goes unremarked, especially at home. Moreover, the recent boom, running roughly from 1990 to 2014, is a surprise—unlike the two earlier booms in the country's history, which were both predictable, although for different reasons, and easy to explain.

This book went on to explore the cultural and social factors that have acted in combination with economic ones, to enable high prosperity. In regard to the necessary cultural preconditions, an assembly of four themes was singled out: Australian cities, civic culture, the national myth, and nature. Within this quartet, it has been the vitality of the cities that has been the main chemical ingredient in the crucible of prosperity, with the other three factors acting as the cultural agents facilitating combustion.

The cities are where the people live and where most of the

nation's economic activity is generated—the exception being farming. Even mining is planned, driven, and managed out of offices based in the cities (one-third of Western Australian mining jobs are in Perth). The metropolis is the engine room of contemporary economic dynamism, as it is throughout the developed world. Moreover, cities that function well, and that are pleasant places in which to live, complement the contemporary economy, which has the service sector as its main organ—symbolised by the importance of creative industries.

Australia has become very good at cities—building ones that combine liveability with economic dynamism. This is a rare achievement, one of inestimable benefit in the context of the argument of this book. While cities are central to economic vitality in every developed country today, Australia has managed to create ones of special contemporary quality. This is an achievement recognised internationally, with Melbourne merely slightly ahead of the others in being ranked the world's most liveable city, the world's friendliest city, and the world's Ultimate Sport City. Sydney was recently ranked the world's most beautiful large city.

How has this happened? The British cultural gene has somehow adapted to a new social environment in which there is much less consciousness of class, and a less rigid and vertical status hierarchy; and to a physical environment in which there is plentiful space and a more temperate climate. The inhabitants have fostered a way of living in closer proximity to nature and the elements; they have learnt how to utilise the outdoors. Parisian and Roman street culture has been imported in recent decades, in adapted antipodean form—with cafés, bars, restaurants, and local markets proliferating in the inner cities. Large-scale multi-cultural immigration has injected energy, resourcefulness, and broadened the human landscape. An ethos of ready movement in space has extrapolated, encouraging enterprise, and mobility in life.

The success of the cities in the post-War period has depended on high levels of multicultural immigration, the porosity of local institutions, the development of a suburban lifestyle that is attractive to families, high geographical and social mobility within cities, and a resulting rapid assimilation of the new Australians—no ethnic ghettoes have emerged. The continuation of this tradition will be indispensable to future prosperity.

The Australian success at cities is linked to a civic culture of respect for authority, and a liking for order. It has combined with a practical democratic temper, with its own emphasis on giving everyone a fair go, tolerance of diversity as long as people fit in, and a pervasive scepticism about militant beliefs and ideologues. A disposition for hard work has strengthened in recent decades, and contributed to high social mobility, and an optimistic confidence that the conditions of life, both for individuals and collectively, can be improved. This culture was highlighted in the Bradman style: *Never uninteresting—abstaining from vanity and rhetoric.*

Innovative economic dynamism and the broader civic culture have somehow developed in harmony, feeding each other with a kind of symbiotic cross-fertilization. It is here that the 'lucky country' ascription may have some cogency.

A national myth is still developing, concurrently pitched at two levels. There is the collective city story, with its key chapters focussed on suburban domesticity and urban cosmopolitanism. A body of narratives that reflects this reality remains in an embryonic state. We may anticipate development on this front, with the emergence of domestic equivalents to Edward Hopper, John Updike, and *The Sopranos*; and hopefully ones pitched in a more life-affirming key.

And there is an epic, supra-historical body of narrative. Like the cities, it has taken generations to reach maturity. The Anzac legend complements the suburban/urban story in that it is the ordinary soldiers who are celebrated, not singular individual heroes. The composite myth that results serves to give legitimacy, to reinforce a sense of meaning and purpose, and to boost morale and self-belief.

The very status of the myth as a work-in-progress contributes to the sense of a nation still in the making. It operates today, unlike in the more distant past, among a people who have enough security in how things are, that the projected myths do not need to be defensive and compensatory. Those myths are freer to articulate truths, contribute to self-understanding, and give shape and flesh to identity.

Nature is the secular divinity that rules the land. It helps to earth the inhabitants. I have suggested that the ambivalences it imposes may explain a paradox at the core of the nation's character, that the pleasant and sociable habitats within which the people live and work do not encourage careless indolence, but rather a seriousness about life, and a drive to take it on.

Nature, in its punitive mode, tests human endurance and provides cautionary tales about complacency, over-weening pride, and high ambition. In its benevolent mode, it succours and blesses. It is as if the gods are ever-near, with their presence and their power displaced into a natural backdrop on which scenes play out, ones ranging from sublime beauty and benign calm, to storm and fated catastrophe. The human dwellers find themselves flitting through these scenes, the naive actors cast in a drama not of their own choosing. At their best, they manage to live in a way that is never uninteresting, but abstaining from vanity and rhetoric.

Les Murray brought his own rural sensibility into the centre of the city in his poem *An Absolutely Ordinary Rainbow*, prefiguring the 2014 Sydney Siege, which would occur four decades later. A man is crying in Martin Place, cocooned in a 'pentagram of sorrow', the dignity of his weeping holding the gathering crowd back:

*Some will say, in the years to come, a halo
or force stood around him. There is no such thing.
Some will say they were shocked and would have stopped him
but they will not have been there. The fiercest manhood,
the toughest reserve, the slickest wit amongst us*

*trembles with silence, and burns with unexpected
judgements of peace. Some in the concourse scream
who thought themselves happy. Only the smallest children
and such as look out of Paradise come near him
and sit at his feet, with dogs and dusty pigeons.*

A mood something like this rose in Sydney during the siege, transmuted into an outpouring of grief in the aftermath, as thousands left flowers at an impromptu memorial. The poet's prescience had been uncanny, his art giving a timeless clarity of form and an emotional gravity to the bewildered shock and sorrow that shadowed this tragedy.

Martin Place happens to be where Sydney's Anzac Day march begins—the nation's myth also serving to prefigure the Siege story. That story, as it was told later via television documentary, played in a different major key. It glowed with the presence of two 19-year-old students who had moved with a canny and selfless, heroic calm through sixteen hours of terror. They were to recount the events with sober reflection, eloquent beyond their years, sadly thoughtful while displaying the cheerful resilience that had sustained them on the day. Vanity and rhetoric were absent. These students are the hope of the future.

The *Economist's* special report on Australia in 2011 was subtitled 'With a bit of self-belief, Australia could become a model nation'. The argument of this book has attempted to give concrete form, amongst other things, to the notion of 'self-belief'—in itself rather vague. It has found the constituent elements of that self-belief in the civic culture, supported by the nation's myths, and articulated through modern city life. Here are lodged the antibodies to insecure identity. Further, what is in the fabric of the people and their culture, within the domain of their authority and their optimism, has generally been picked up in the leadership elites, but not always, and translated into astute policy. That same authority will need reasserting over bureaucracy and the vanity of its proliferations; keeping administration subservient to the real tasks and goals of whichever organisation it serves.

What have we learnt about the key to economic growth, and to prosperity? Have we been able to flesh out the metaphor of *animal spirits*; and to become more explicit than the evocative but airy notions of metropolitan *buzz*, *fizz*, and a *special kind of energy*?

When we view Australia from a historical perspective the contribution of the rural sector and that of the outback stand out: wool and gold; followed by wheat, lamb, and beef; and now coal, gas, and iron-ore. But the balance has shifted. While these agricultural products and natural resources, once the foundation of Australian prosperity, do today remain a powerful supporting cast, the gold of the new, post-war Australia is lodged in the cities. It is formed out of the culture of the people.

That takes us to the mystery of the cities, one of the twin foci of this book. The Australian talent for building contemporary cities has depended on a broad economy, so that some sectors rise when others fall, providing a general cushioning during recessed periods, and diverse sources of surging enterprise in buoyant times. It has depended on large-scale and continuous, multi-cultural immigration, injecting a diversity of energy, ideas, and entrepreneurial initiative. It has depended on the topography of the different cities, and how they have exploited and developed their natural advantages, and with extended reference to the local climate. It has depended, finally, on the suburbs and their own social topography centred on families; and the way they have interacted, in recent decades, with a contrasting urban cosmopolitanism.

These four factors have, in turn, depended for their fulfilment on a number of conditions. There has been, first and foremost, able civic leadership—that is, political and administrative elites with a capacity for visionary planning and the wherewithal to put plans into practice. One offshoot is a public domain dotted with examples of excellence—in buildings, public spaces, and crafted natural landscapes; in galleries and museums, scientific research and artistic creation; in organisations and events; in sport; and in shops, bars, restaurants and cafés. Excellence sets a standard and a tone. It is always under threat.

There has been the critical role played by a civic culture that is tolerant and open, welcoming waves of poly-ethnic immigrants in their millions, and assimilating them with comparative ease, as long as they make some effort to fit in. An aspect of that civic culture is concern for the education of children, and a linked interest in the quality of schools.

If the key to where people want to go—to live and to work—has shifted from where the companies and the industries are based to location, then the new urban cosmopolitanism that has emerged since 1990 is vital. In explaining prosperity, it is as important as civic leadership. And, as we have seen, the two belong together, with leadership essential to the development of liveable cities. Knowledge-intensive and creative industries will determine future prosperity, and they are, of their nature, drawn to cosmopolitan inner-city milieus.

The single major change in Australian life since 1990, when the country's third economic boom got under way, has been the metamorphosis of the inner cities. The efflorescence of the inner urban—with CBDs transformed from dead centres into throbbing hearts—has emerged hand-in-hand with current prosperity. Cause and effect are blurred. While urban cosmopolitanism would not have developed in a flat economy, it is equally the case that a vibrant urban society, including its environs, attracts knowledge-intensive industry. There is mutual stimulation and support at work here.

Urbanity goes with mobility. A dynamic and liveable city works off several dualisms. Friction and stress alternate with serenity and composure, as in a volatile climate plunging from storm into calm, and back to storm again. At one pole, there is fluidity, motion, and transience, all with the eye cast internationally; at the other pole, attachment to the local. Adventurousness goes hand in hand with mobility, and the freedom to roam physically and imaginatively. Paradoxically, it is enabled by engagement with familiar and loved places. When a city is succeeding, secure roots in the local liberate rather than constrain.

Australia as it is known today is largely a post World-War-Two entity. The half-century of economic stagnation between 1890 and 1940, viewed in retrospect, appears to have served like a lost, wayward period of adolescence—leaving aside the political importance of Federation, and that this period saw the birth of the Anzac myth. Considering the seventy-year stretch since the war, the cities have only in the later part become truly metropolitan. Their look and feel now is very different from even that of their 1970s and 1980s selves. It has been like a coming of age, one that has been long in gestation.

Whether or not what we currently experience is the mature form, we have gained a clearer snapshot of the full potential. 'Mature form' is a term that can only be used loosely, for a modern economy, like the society it helps shape, is in a constant state of flux—that economy's driving principle being 'creative destruction', as described by Marx, and later Schumpeter. More accurately put, we have gained a clearer picture of the framework of success, in reading how the cities as living organisms now breathe, think, and grow. Also, we have located some of the means for furthering that success.

ACKNOWLEDGEMENTS

I am indebted to conversations with Rob Adams (Director of City Design, City of Melbourne), Peter Beilharz (sociologist), Alison Carroll, Mike Clayton (golf professional, course designer, and writer), Peter Corrigan (architect), Glyn Davis (Vice-Chancellor, Melbourne University), Richard Gill (conductor, music director and educator), John Hirst (historian), Philip Hunter (artist), Sara James (sociologist), Anthony Moran (sociologist), Peter Murphy, Alan Stockdale (former Victorian Treasurer), Leon van Schaik (Professor of Innovative Architecture, Royal Melbourne Institute of Technology), Nick Shelton (Director and Publisher, *Broadsheet Media*), and John Timlin. Alison Carroll, Glyn Davis, Richard Gill, Sara James, and John Timlin were particularly generous with their comments. And, I am deeply indebted to my wife Eva—as always, and in many ways.

BIBLIOGRAPHY

Rob Adams, *Postcode 3000, A City Transformed?* City of Melbourne, 2013.

Jaynie Anderson, *Tiepolo's Cleopatra*, Macmillan, Melbourne, 2003.

Hannah Arendt, *On Revolution*, Faber & Faber, London, 1964.

Reyner Banham, *Los Angeles, The Architecture of Four Ecologies*, Penguin, London, 1971.

C. E. W. Bean, *The Official History of Australia in the War of 1914-1918*, Angus and Robertson, Sydney, 1937, vol. V.

Geoffrey Blainey, *A Land Half Won*, Macmillan, Melbourne, 1980.

Geoffrey Blainey, *The Steel Master*, Macmillan, Melbourne, 1971.

Geoffrey Blainey, *The Story of Australia's People, The Rise and Rise of a New Australia*, Penguin, Melbourne, 2016.

James Boyce, *1835: The Founding of Melbourne and the Conquest of Australia*, Black Inc., Melbourne, 2012.

Calypso Summer, Australian Broadcasting Corporation Video, 2000.

John Carroll, *Greek Pilgrimage*, Scribe, Melbourne, 2010.

John Carroll, *The Western Dreaming*, Harper Collins, Sydney, 2001.

Nick Cater, *The Lucky Culture*, Harper Collins, Sydney, 2013.

John Clarke, *Sporting Nation*, Australian Broadcasting Commission DVD, 2012.

Mike Clayton, *The Courses of the Royal Melbourne Golf Club*, Melbourne University Press, Melbourne, 2011.

Inga Clendinnan, *Dancing with Strangers*, Canongate, London, 2005.

Michael Clyne & James Jupp, ed., *Multiculturalism and Integration: A Harmonious Relationship*, ANU Press, Canberra, 2011.

Hal Colebatch, *Australia's Secret War: How Unionists Sabotaged our Troops in World War II*, Quadrant Books, Melbourne, 2013.

Land of the Golden Cities

Ronald Conway, *The Great Australian Stupor*, Sun Books, Melbourne, 1971.

Ronald Conway, *Land of the Long Weekend*, Sun Books, Melbourne, 1978.

A. F. Davies, *Australian Democracy*, Longmans, Melbourne, 1958.

Graeme Davison, *Car Wars: how the car won our hearts and conquered our cities*, Allen & Unwin, Sydney, 2004.

Graeme Davison, *The Rise and Fall of Marvellous Melbourne*, Melbourne University Press, Melbourne, 1978.

David De Vaus, *Diversity and Change in Australian Families*, Australian Institute of Family Studies, Melbourne, 2004.

Emile Durkheim, *Suicide, a Study in Sociology*, trans. John A. Spaulding and George Simpson, Routledge & Kegan Paul, London, 1952.

Sue Ebury, *Weary*, Penguin, Melbourne, 1995.

Niall Ferguson, *Civilisation*, Allen Lane, London, 2011.

Richard Florida, *The Rise of the Creative Class, Revisited*, Basic Books, New York, 2012.

Bill Gammage, *The Broken Years*, Penguin, Melbourne, 1975.

Nathan Glazer and Daniel P. Moynihan, *Beyond the Melting Pot*, MIT Press, Boston, 1970.

Peter Hall, *Cities in Civilization*, Weidenfeld & Nicolson, London, 1998.

HILDA Survey 2011: Families, Incomes and Jobs, vol. 6, Melbourne Institute of Applied Economic and Social Research.

HILDA Survey 2014, Families, Incomes and Jobs, vol. 9, ed. Roger Wilkins, Melbourne Institute of Applied Economic and Social Research.

John Hirst, *Sense and Nonsense in Australian History*, Black Inc, Melbourne 2005.

Kenneth Hopper and William Hopper, *The Puritan Gift, Reclaiming the American Dream amidst Global Financial Chaos*, I. B. Tauris, New York, 2007.

Donald Horne, *The Lucky Country*, Penguin, Melbourne, 1964.

Robert Hughes, *The Art of Australia*, Penguin, Melbourne, 1965.

Robert Hughes, *The Fatal Shore*, Collins Harvill, London, 1986.

Australia's Exceptional Prosperity and the Culture that Made It

K. S. Inglis, *Sacred Places*, Miegunyah, Melbourne, 1998.

Jane Jacobs, *The Death and Life of Great American Cities*, Jonathan Cape, London, 1962.

Jane Jacobs, *The Economy of Cities*, Random House, New York, 1969.

Howard Jacobson, *Brilliant Creatures*, ABC TV Documentary, 2014.

Sara James, *Making a Living, Making a Life: Contemporary Narratives of Work, Vocation and Meaning*, Routledge, London, forthcoming 2017.

Jane-Frances Kelly and Paul Donegan, *Mapping Australia's Economy, Cities as Engines of Prosperity*, Grattan Institute, July 2014.

Jane-Frances Kelly and Peter Mares, *Productive Cities*, Grattan Institute, May 2013.

Paul Kelly, *The March of the Patriots—The Struggle for Modern Australia*, Melbourne University Press, Melbourne, 2009.

Rod Kemp and Marion Stanton (eds.), *Speaking for Australia, Parliamentary speeches that shaped our nation*, Allen & Unwin, Sydney, 2004.

Charles Landry, *The Art of City Making*, Earthscan, London, 2006.

Tim Low, *Where Song Began, Australian birds and how they changed the world*, Penguin, Melbourne, 2014.

Ian W. McLean, *Why Australia Prospered*, Princeton University Press, Princeton, 2013.

George Megalogenis, *Making Australia Great: Inside Our Longest Boom*, ABC TV documentary, 2015.

Jonathan Mills (ed.), *The Alfred Deakin Lectures*, ABC Books, Sydney, 2001.

John Murphy, *Imagining the Fifties*, University of New South Wales Press, Sydney, 2000.

Peter Murphy, *The Creative Wasteland of Post-Industrial Society*, Ashgate, London, 2015.

Peter Murphy, *The Collective Imagination, The Creative Spirit of Free Societies*, Ashgate, London, 2012.

Friedrich Nietzsche, *The Birth of Tragedy*, trans. Walter Kaufmann, Modern Library, New York, 1968.

Mikalya Novak and Dom Talimanidis, *Things are getting better all the time*, Institute of Public Affairs, Melbourne, October 2014.

J. Pincus and G. Hugo (eds.), *A greater Australia, population, policies, and governance*, CEDA, Melbourne, 2012.

Robert Putnam, *Bowling Alone*, Simon & Schuster, New York, 2000.

Saskia Sassen, *The Global City*, Princeton University Press, Princeton, 1991.

Leon van Schaik, *Design City Melbourne*, Wiley-Academy, London, 2006.

Joseph Schumpeter, *Capitalism, Socialism and Democracy*, George Allen & Unwin, London, 1954.

George Steiner, *No Passion Spent*, Yale University Press, New Haven, 1996.

Craig Taylor, *Londoners*, Granta, London, 2011.

Clinton Walker, *History is Made at Night: Live Music in Australia*, Platform Papers, Currency House, Sydney, July 2012.

Russel Ward, *The Australian Legend*, Oxford University Press, Melbourne, 1958.

Don Watson, *The Bush*, Penguin, Melbourne, 2014.

Max Weber, *The Protestant Ethic and the Spirit of Capitalism*, trans. Talcott Parsons, Unwin, London, 1930.

Patrick Weller and James Cutt, *Treasury Control in Australia*, Ian Novak, Sydney, 1976.

Richard White, *On Holidays*, Pluto Press, Melbourne, 2005.

NOTES

Prologue

[1] Interview, *The Australian*, 28 March, 2015.
[2] The case is thoroughly documented by Possum Comitatus in 'Australian Exceptionalism', *Crikey.com*, December 8, 2011.
[3] *Economist*, May 28, 2011, Special Report titled 'No Worries?' leader titled 'The next Golden State'.
[4] Max Weber, *The Protestant Ethic and the Spirit of Capitalism*.
[5] John Carroll, 'The Role of Guilt in the Formation of Modern Society: England 1350-1800', *The British Journal of Sociology*, vol. 32, no. 4, December 1981.

1. An Extraordinary Economy

[6] HILDA Survey 2014, Families, Incomes and Jobs.
[7] Figures sourced in Possum Comitatus, and the *Economist*, op. cit.
[8] *Australian Jobs 2011*, Australian Government Department of Education, Employment, and Workplace Relations.
[9] HILDA Survey 2014.
[10] Increasing alienation at work is argued, for instance, by Richard Sennett, in his 1998 book *Corrosion of Character: The Personal Consequences of Work in the New Capitalism* (Norton, New York).
[11] HILDA Survey 2011: Families, Incomes and Jobs.
[12] Andrew Leigh and Justin Wolfers, 'Happiness and the Human Development Index: Australia is not a paradox', *Australian Economic Review*, vol. 39, no. 2, June 2006, p. 176.
[13] Ian W. McLean, *Why Australia Prospered*, p. 32.
[14] Ibid.
[15] Ibid., p. 242.
[16] Ibid., ch. 4.
[17] Ibid., p. 86.
[18] Ibid., ch. 9.
[19] Australian Government Productivity Commission, International Productivity Comparisons, September 2008.
[20] Quoted in Paul Kelly, *The March of the Patriots*, p. 275.

21 Jane Jacobs, *The Economy of Cities*.
22 Jane-Frances Kelly and Paul Donegan, *Mapping Australia's Economy, Cities as Engines of Prosperity*, p. 1.
23 Richard Florida, *The Rise of the Creative Class, Revisited*, pp. 188 and 299. This revised edition responds to critics of the 'creative class' thesis, of which there have been many. Whilst Florida likely pushes his thesis too far, and he writes with an evangelical tone that may jar, he is on to something. This is supported in the wider literature on creative and innovative cities and regions, led by city historians such as Peter Hall (*Cities in Civilization*).
24 Peter Murphy, *The Collective Imagination, The Creative Spirit of Free Societies*; B. Bishop and M. Lisheron, 'Why a city thrives: a mix of open minds', *American Statesman*, 31 December, 2002; J. Kotkin, 'California Suggests Suicide; Texas Asks: Can I lend You a Knife?' *Forbes.com*, November 15, 2010; Jane Jacobs, *The Economy of Cities*; Richard Florida; and especially Peter Hall, pp. 938, 961-989.
25 Murphy, pp. 187-92.
26 Florida, p. 401.
27 Hall, p. 963.
28 Peter Hall tentatively supports the global city argument, ch. 30.
29 For an overview of leading theories of innovation, Hall, ch. 16.
30 Charles Landry, *The Art of City Making*, p. 328.

2 The Australian City: Melbourne Case-Study

31 John Murphy, *Imagining the Fifties*, especially chs. 1 and 5.
32 Richard White, *On Holidays*, ch. 5.
33 Grattan Institute Report, July 2014, p.5.
34 'Greater Melbourne, Method of travel to work', *profile.id.*
35 Graeme Davison, *The Rise and Fall of Marvellous Melbourne*, ch. 7.
36 Ibid., ch. 8.
37 *Enterprise Melbourne*, City of Melbourne.
38 Positioning Australia for Prosperity? Catching the Next Wave, Deloitte Touche Tomatsu, Sydney, 2013.
39 Leon van Schaik, *Design City Melbourne*.
40 Leon van Schaik, Geoffrey London, with Beth George, *Procuring Innovative Architecture*, Routledge, Oxford, 2010.

41 Clinton Walker, *History is Made at Night: Live Music in Australia*.
42 *Countdown*, 2-part ABC television documentary, November 2014.
43 Ibid., p. 45.
44 Notably the *Gin Palace*, *Eau de Vie Melbourne*, *Lily Blacks*, *Golden Monkey*, *Double Happiness*, the *Supper Club*, and *Black Pearl* in Fitzroy. *Eau de Vie* has won multiple international and Australian awards; Lily Blacks won Victorian Bar of the Year in 2013.
45 Hans Westerbeek, 'Melbourne sports capital of the world?', *The Age*, August 12, 2014.
46 'Melbourne beats Sydney in American students' Google searches for overseas universities', *The Age*, 15 February, 2015.
47 Geoffrey Blainey, *The Steel Master*.
48 Deirdre Macken, 'Living the dream, but not buying real estate', *The Australian*, Saturday June 25, 2016.
49 HILDA Survey 2014, ch13.
50 The 2011 Census shows 154,000 claiming to be of whole or part Greek ancestry. This significantly underestimates the actual number, as many second and third generation Greek-Australians designate their ancestry as 'Australian'. The actual Greek ancestry figure may be anything from 200,000 to 300,000.
51 Graeme Hugo: 'Social inclusion and multiculturalism', in J. Pincus and G. Hugo (eds.) *A greater Australia, population, policies, and governance*.
52 Siew-Ean Khoo, 'Intermarriage, Integration and Multiculturalism: A Demographic Perspective', in Michael Clyne & James Jupp, ed., *Multiculturalism and Integration: A Harmonious Relationship*, pp. 111-112.
53 'A Family Affair: Intergenerational Social Mobility across OECD Countries', *Economic Policy Reforms, Going for Growth*, OECD, 2010.
54 John Clarke, *Sporting Nation*, episode 2.
55 Hall, ch. 6.
56 Friedrich Nietzsche, *The Birth of Tragedy*.
57 Rob Adams, *Postcode 3000, A City Transformed?*
58 'Skyscraper warning for postcode 3000', *The Age*, August 20, 2013.
59 *The Streets of Melbourne, From Early Photographs*, The Herald and Weekly Times, Melbourne, 1987.
60 John Carroll, *Greek Pilgrimage*, p. 61.
61 Bernard Salt, *The Australian*, 11-7-2013.

62. For a detailed pictorial and analytical analysis of Royal Melbourne's design quality see Mike Clayton, *The Courses of the Royal Melbourne Golf Club*.
63. Jaynie Anderson, *Tiepolo's Cleopatra*, p. 9.
64. John Carroll, 'Reading the Melbourne Poussin', *Quadrant*, May 2016.
65. Donald Horne, *The Lucky Country*, p. 220.
66. Ronald Conway, *The Great Australian Stupor*, p. 262.
67. 'Limey! The world agrees: Oz the place to be', *The Australian*, 19 August, 2013.
68. 'From Fitzroy to Flatbush', *Broadsheet Melbourne*, 21 July, 2014.
69. Reyner Banham, *Los Angeles*.
70. Jane-Frances Kelly and Peter Mares, *Productive Cities*, p. 12.
71. 'Our Liveable City', *The (Melbourne) magazine*, *The Age*, Issue 86, December 2011.
72. Melbourne has its own Chandler equivalents, in the crime thrillers of Peter Temple and Shane Maloney. Plenty of local urban description and attachment colour Temple's *White Dog* (2003), for example, but the style is derivative from Chandler, while lacking the charm and easy flair. Maloney writes more smoothly, and his *The Brush-Off* (1996), for example, combines high drama with effective satirizing of Labor politics and the arts world, but it lacks the existential depth of Chandler.
73. Grattan Institute Report, May 2013, p. 34.
74. Jane Jacobs, *The Death and Life of Great American Cities*, Part One.
75. *Bach 2000*, Melbourne Festival, 2000; Jonathan Mills ed., *The Alfred Deakin Lectures*.
76. There were predecessors, such as the 1950s Snowy Mountains Hydroelectric Scheme, and the 1956 Olympics, not to mention large-scale mining projects.
77. Joel Kotkin, *The Next Hundred Million: America in 2050*, Penguin, London, 2010.
78. Craig Taylor (ed.), *Londoners*, pp. 143-8.
79. Saskia Sassen, *The Global City*.
80. Banham, pp. 243-4.

3. The Australian City: Sydney Snapshot

81. Geoffrey Blainey, *The Story of Australia's People*, 2016, p. 62.
82. Donald Horne, *The Lucky Country*, p. 50.
83. Robert Hughes, *The Fatal Shore*, p. 323.

4. Civic Culture

84 The term coined by French sociologist, Emile Durkheim, in his 1897 study of *Suicide*.

85 Around 35% of domestic investment in the period 1861 to 1889 was raised on the London capital markets—it was higher in the 1880s (McLean, p. 105).

86 McLean, pp. 99-100.

87 McLean, p. 161.

88 Kelly, pp. 188-97.

89 Hannah Arendt, *On Revolution*, p. 200.

90 Calypso Summer.

91 John Hirst, *Sense and Nonsense in Australian History*, ch. 1.

92 C. E. W. Bean, *The Official History of Australia in the War of 1914-1918*, vol. V, p. 22.

93 Howard Jacobson, *Brilliant Creatures*.

94 Judith Brett and Anthony Moran, 'Cosmopolitan nationalism: ordinary people making sense of diversity', *Nations and Nationalism*, 17 (1), 2011.

95 Andrew Markus, *Mapping Social Cohesion, the Scanlon Foundation survey 2014*, Monash University, pp. 13-14.

96 Australian Government Department of Transport and Regional Services, *Focus on Regions, No. 4 Social Capital*, Commonwealth of Australia, 2005.

97 I am indebted to John Timlin for this observation.

98 The source is the work of Emile Durkheim, with the most influential recent development of the case in the work of the American sociologist Robert Putnam, and in particular in his 2000 book *Bowling Alone*.

99 John Carroll, 'English riots, 2011: Two comments', *Thesis Eleven*, no. 109, April 2012.

100 Graphically documented in the Victorian case by James Boyce in his book, *1835: The Founding of Melbourne and the Conquest of Australia*.

101 Jacobson.

102 For example, Ronald Conway, *Land of the Long Weekend*, p. 188.

103 Hal Colebatch, *Australia's Secret War: How Unionists Sabotaged our Troops in World War II*.

104 Hilda Survey 2011.

105 E.g. Sara James, *Making a Living, Making a Life: Contemporary Narratives of Work, Vocation and Meaning*, Routledge, London, forthcoming 2017.

Land of the Golden Cities

[106] I am indebted here to a conversation with Peter Murphy.
[107] Exemplified in his famous 1942 broadcast on 'The Forgotten People', delivered in the period in which he was founding the Liberal Party.
[108] As a counter-example, I can attest that at Cambridge in the late 1960s undergraduates were worked much harder than at Melbourne University. Writing three essays every two weeks during term was the norm.
[109] Nathan Glazer and Daniel P. Moynihan, *Beyond the Melting Pot*.

5. The Nation's Myth

[110] Geoffrey Blainey, *A Land Half Won*, p. 360.
[111] Hannah Arendt, *On Revolution*, ch. 5.
[112] Robert N. Bellah, 'Civil Religion in America', *Daedalus,* Winter 1967.
[113] John Hirst, *Sense & Nonsense in Australia History*, p. 251.
[114] Friedrich Nietzsche, *The Birth of Tragedy*, section 23.
[115] John Carroll, *The Western Dreaming*.
[116] Ibid., ch. 3.
[117] Bean, vol. 1, pp. 606-7.
[118] K. S. Inglis, *Sacred Places*.
[119] Sue Ebury, *Weary*.
[120] The argument is put at length by John Clarke in an ABC TV documentary series, *Sporting Nation*, 2012.
[121] Calypso Summer.
[122] Bill Gammage, *The Broken Years*, ch. 2.
[123] 'The Siege Survivors', *60 Minutes*, 8-9 February, 2015.
[124] Geoffrey Blainey, *A Land Half Won*, p. 44.
[125] In *The Western Dreaming*, I have argued that the cultural tradition includes nine archetypal stories, one of which is the hero.
[126] Scott Doidge, *The Anxiety of Ascent—Middle-Class Narratives in Germany and America*, La Trobe University PhD thesis, 2017, ch. 3.
[127] Weekly household expenditure on housing doubled between 1975 and 1997 (David De Vaus, *Diversity and Change in Australian Families*, pp. 274-5).
[128] Ibid., p.140.

6. Nature

[129] Tim Low, *Where Song Began*, p. 2.
[130] Don Watson, *The Bush*, pp. 1-64.
[131] Interview with Aida Edemariam, *The Guardian*, 28 June, 2008.
[132] Chris Wallace-Crabbe, address at a dinner in celebration of his eightieth birthday, University House, Melbourne University, May 16, 2014.
[133] Ronald Conway, *Land of the Long Weekend*. Conway even stresses the little that Australians work compared with Americans and Germans (p. 188).
[134] David Tacey, in lectures at La Trobe University in a course on 'The Crisis of Meaning in the Twenty-First Century'.
[135] Robert Hughes, *The Art of Australia*, p. 35.
[136] Low, p. 87.

7. Threats

[137] Kelly, p. 275.
[138] Ibid., ch. 25.
[139] Christopher Graham Salisbury, *The 'smart' state: building a knowledge economy in Queensland since the 1990s*, PhD thesis, University of Queensland, 2013.
[140] A. F. Davies, *Australian Democracy*.
[141] Peter Shergold, 'Alfred Deakin and the Machinery of Commonwealth Administration', *Quadrant*, May 2014.
[142] Kenneth Hopper and William Hopper, *The Puritan Gift, Reclaiming the American Dream amidst Global Financial Chaos*.
[143] Peter Murphy, *The Cultural Wasteland of Post-Industrial Society*, p. 110. Also, Nicholas Graves, Adrian Barnett, and Philip Clarke, 'Reform Australian universities by cutting their bureaucracies', theconversation.com, March 18, 2013.
[144] *Review of the National Museum of Australia—Its Exhibitions and Public Programs*, Department of Communications, Information Technology and the Arts, Commonwealth of Australia, July 2003.
[145] For a balanced view of the Treasury in an earlier generation, see Patrick Weller and James Cutt, *Treasury Control in Australia*, pp. 151-2.
[146] Jerry Pournelle, *The View from Chaos Manor*, April 3, 2006.
[147] Joseph Schumpeter, *Capitalism, Socialism and Democracy*, pp. 133-5.
[148] George Steiner, *No Passion Spent*, pp. 304-27.
[149] Niall Ferguson, *Civilisation*, p. 212.
[150] Steiner, pp. 88-107.

INDEX

Abbott, Tony, 151
Adams, Rob, 47, 49, 67
Adelaide, 20, 27, 49, 73, 75, 103-4, 134, 158
America, United States, 5, 7, 9, 11, 12-13, 19, 25, 44, 61, 87, 89, 91-2, 98, 109-10, 114, 119-20, 122, 133, 163-4
Amor, Rick, 31
ANZAC, creation myth, 88, 112-16, 119, 122-8, 131-2, 150, 166, 172, 176
Aphrodite, 127
Arendt, Hannah, 109-10, 114
Aristotle, 107
Arnold, Matthew, 136
Athena, 127, 131
Augustine, 110
Australia, gold rushes, 16-17, 18; post-1990 boom, 6-10, 11-23, 169; wellbeing, 14
Australian Ballet, 32
Australian Broadcasting Commission (ABC), 74, 75, 83
Australian Dream, 5
Australian football, AFL, 35-7, 50, 62-3, 101, 120, 123
Australian Research Council (ARC), 157
Australian War Memorial, 114, 116, 125, 144

Bach, Johann Sebastian, 22, 63
Ballard, J. G., 47
Balzac, 22
Banham, Reyner, 58, 67
Barassi, Ron, 94-5
Barry, Redmond, 48
Baynton, Barbara, 56, 133
Beach, 5, 69-70, 135-7, 142, 144, 146-7

Bean, C. E. W., 112-13, 116, 126, 150
Beattie, Peter, 153-4
Bellah, Robert, 110
Benaud, Richie, 90, 97, 116
Beresford, Bruce, 77
BHP Billiton, 12, 28
Blainey, Geoffrey, 20, 108-9, 149-50
Booth, Peter, 31
Boston, 110
Boyd, Arthur, 31, 56, 133
Boyd, Robin, 55, 60
Bradman, Don, 97, 116-8, 150, 171
Brisbane, 27, 49, 68, 76, 82, 99, 119, 134, 153-4, 158
Broadsheet Melbourne, 54
Bulletin, The, 76
Bureaucratic rationalism, 97, 138-9, 145, 154-61, 174
Burgess, Gregory, 30
Burke and Wills, 133, 152
Bush, George W., 122
Bushfires, 134, 148

Cahill, Joseph, 72
Cain, John, 47
Calwell, Arthur, 17
Calypso Summer, West Indies cricket team, 90, 95, 116-17, 120
Canada, 11, 20, 44, 92
Canberra, 76, 84, 122, 123, 134, 147, 152, 153, 156
Cardus, Neville, 150
Carlyon, Les, 126
Castle, The, 60, 132, 144
Cave, Nick, 71, 121
Chamberlain, Lindy, 146

Chandler, Raymond, 60
Chifley, Ben, 17
China, 7, 19, 87, 164
Churchill, Winston, 166
Cities, 9-10, 19-23, 25-80, 81, 131, 169-71, 174-7
Civic culture, 81-105, 169, 171, 175; authority, 84-8, 171; English influence, 81-4, 97, 98, 102, 103, 109, 127, 138, 161-7, 171; democratic temper, 83, 88-97, 148, 171; work, 98-105, 171
Civic leadership, 47-8, 50, 67, 72, 149-54, 162, 174, 175
Clark, Manning, 111
Conway, Ronald, 55, 137
Corrigan, Peter, 30
Cricket, 38, 46, 90, 95, 116-18, 120
Crocodile Dundee, 9
Cronulla riots, 95-6
Crowe, Russell, 132

Darwin, 152-3
Davis Cup, 119
Davis, Glyn, 34
Davies, A. F., 154
Deakinite Settlement, 91
Demetriou, Andrew, 45
Demography, 13-14, 129, 135
DiPierdomenico, Robert, 45
Dobell, William, 78
Dream, The, Roy and HG, 89, 92, 96, 98, 144
Drysdale, Russell, 76-7, 133
Dunlop, Edward 'Weary', 113, 116

Echidna, 139-40, 144
Education, 101-2, 155-8, 175
English language, 92, 165-6
Entrepreneurs, 40-43, 175

European Union, 162, 163, 165, 167
Evans, Cadel, 121

Father Knows Best, 128
Florida, Richard, 20-21, 60
Ford, John, 127; The Searchers, 133
France, French, 13, 44, 86, 138, 166
Freeman, Cathy, 95, 96
Freud, 117

Germany, German, 14, 166
Gibson, Mel, 132
Gillard, Julia, 130, 150
Glover, John, 56
Godsell, Sean, 30
Golf, 52, 120-21
Goss, Wayne, 153
Greece, classical Greece, 12, 43, 50-51, 67, 97, 111-12, 114-16, 131, 135, 140, 162-3
Greeley, Horace, 133
Griffith Review, 154
Griffith University, 154, 158

Hall, Peter, 21-2, 29, 46
Hall, Wes, 117
Hawke, Robert, 17, 75, 99, 100-101, 103, 124, 157
Henson, Bill, 31
Henry, Ken, 18, 160
Hewitt, Lleyton, 97
Hibberd, Jack, 33
High culture, 166
Hirst, John, 90-91
Hobbes, 84, 85
Hoddle, Robert, 48
Hoff, Rayner, 113
Holt, Harold, 146-7
Home, as ideal, 128-32

Hong Kong, 83, 103, 152, 153, 164, 166
Hope, A. D., 56
Hopper, Edward, 171
Hopper, Kenneth and William, 154-5, 157
Horne, Donald, 55, 78, 98, 149
Howard, John, 75, 76, 88-9, 100-101, 103, 122
Hughes, Robert, 79, 92, 124-5
Humphries, Barry, 56, 78, 92, 96, 145
Hunte, Conrad, 117
Hunter, Philip, 31

Iliad, The, Homer, 111-12, 114-15, 126, 147-8, 166
Indigenous Australians, 96, 139, 142-3, 145
Industrial Revolution, 19, 81-2
Inglis, Ken, 115
Irwin, Steve, 134, 146

Jacobs, Jane, 19
James, Clive, 5, 79-80, 92
Japan, 164
Jesus, Lives of, 111

Keating, Paul, 75, 99
Kelly, Paul, 87, 149
Kelty, Bill, 99
Kemp, C. D., 116
Kennett, Jeff, 47-8
Keynes, John Maynard, 20, 22, 160
Kotkin, Joel, 64

Landry, Charles, 23
Lasch, Christopher, 129
La Trobe, Charles, 48
La Trobe University, 45
Laver, Rod, 97

Lawrence, D. H., 54-5
Lawson, Henry, 75, 76
Leak, Bill, 78, 97
Lette, Kathy, 97
Leunig, Michael, 96-7, 138
Lewis, Essington, 41
Li Na, 95
Lilley, Chris, 96
Lindrum, Walter, 118
London, 49, 54, 57, 64-5, 71, 82, 83, 102
Longstaff, Will, 114, 115, 125
Los Angeles, 64, 67
Luhrmann, Baz, 77

Malouf, David, 75
Martin Place siege, 93-4, 121, 173-4
Marx, 177
McCarthy, Cormac, 131
Macfarlane, Ian, 149
Mackeller, Dorothea, 136
Mclean, Ian, 15-19, 82, 149, 152
Megalogenis, George, 7
Melbourne, 19, 20, 23, 25-68, 72, 73, 74, 76, 104, 108, 122, 134, 146, 149, 158, 170; Botanic Gardens, 52-3; Crown Casino, 51-52; Docklands, 51; economy, 28-42, 66; golf sand belt, 52; immigration, 28, 42-6, 66, 68, 171, 175; Museum, 53; National Gallery (NGV), 50, 53; suburbs, 25-6, 28, 58-64, 66; topography, 28, 46-57, 66; urban cosmopolitanism, 5, 26, 28, 58-64, 66, 68, 175, 176;
Melbourne Cricket Ground (MCG), 36-7, 93, 104
Melbourne Olympics, 119
Melbourne University, 34, 38-40, 60, 156
Meldrum, Molly, 33-4
Menzies, Robert, 17, 75, 100-101, 103, 154

Michels, Robert, 160, 161
Miller, George, 77, 159; Babe, 132; Mad Max, 77, 133-4
Mills, Jonathan, 63
Monash, John, 127
Murdoch, Rupert, 41, 43
Muriel's Wedding, 132
Murphy, Peter, 21, 155
Murray, Les, *An Absolutely Ordinary Rainbow,* 173

Nation's myth, 107-32, 169, 171-2
National Museum of Australia, 114, 158-9
Nature, as cultural influence, 133-48, 169, 172
Ned Kelly, 133
Neighbourliness, 62, 93-4, 95
Netherlands, 11
New York, 57, 65
New Zealand, 46, 68, 92, 111, 120
Nietzsche, 47, 111
Nolan, Sidney, 31, 56, 124, 133
Norway, 11

OECD, 11-12, 13, 18, 19, 44, 151, 152
Owen, Wilfred, 126

Paris, 22, 46, 57, 64-5, 163, 170
Park, Ruth, *The Muddle-headed Wombat,* 145
Patterson, Banjo, 76
Perth, 49, 68, 73, 170
Phillips, A. A., 55
Plato, 107
Popular culture, 25, 71, 128-30
Porter, Michael, 15
Pournelle, Jerry, 161

Qantas, 145

Rafter, Pat, 97
Rand, Ayn, 13
River cities, 48-9, 104
RMIT, 30, 60-61, 158
Roberts, Tom, 56, 141
Rome, ancient Romans, 90, 110, 163, 165, 170
Rudd, Kevin, 101, 150, 160

Saarinen, Eero, 72
Sassoon, Siegfried, 126
Schaik, Leon van, 29, 30
Schumpeter, Joseph, 15, 161, 177
Scott, Adam, 97, 121
Shakespeare, 84-5, 97, 166
Simpson, the Man with the Donkey, 115
Singapore, 87, 103, 119, 152, 164, 166
Social mobility, 44
Soorley, Jim, 153
Sopranos, The, 171
South Africa, 84
Spooner, John, 97, 136
Sport, 35-8, 48-9, 62-3, 70, 94-5, 98, 116-21
Streeton, Arthur, 56, 141, 142, 145
Steiner, George, 163, 166
Switzerland, 6
Sydney, 19, 20, 23, 27, 31, 33, 38, 44, 48, 51, 69-80, 89-90, 93-4, 108, 134, 143, 170, 173-4; Harbour Bridge, 72, 79; immigration, 73; landscape, 69-70
Sydney Olympics, 63-4, 78, 89-90, 95, 96, 134, 150
Sydney Opera House, 53, 70, 72, 144

Tacey, David, 139

Tasmania, Hobart, 41-42, 73, 75, 103
Taylor, Mark 'Tubby', 117-18, 140
Tennis, 37, 119
Thatcher, Margaret, 100
Thomson, Peter, 119
Tocqueville, Alexis de, 19, 88
Tokyo, 65
Tourism, 38, 74
Trade Unions, 29, 98-9, 100
Treasury, Department of, 159-60
Turnbull, Malcolm, 10, 75, 151

United Kingdom, Britain, 9, 11, 12, 13, 44, 71, 85-6, 92, 96, 100, 111, 119-20, 123, 162-6, 170-71
Universities, 155-7, 159
Updike, John, 171
Utzon, Joern, 72

Veliz, Claudio, 81

Wallace-Crabbe, Chris, 136-7
Warne, Shane, 102
Watson, Don, 124, 135
Weber, Max, 8-9
Weir, Peter, 77, 127, 134, 143, 159; *Picnic at Hanging Rock*, 77, 134, 143; *The Last Wave*, 77, 143
Wellington, Duke of, 165
White, Patrick, 56, 77, 108, 124, 137; *Riders in the Chariot*, 142; *Voss*, 77, 108, 124, 133, 137, 142
Whitlam, Gough, 123
Williams, Fred, 31
Williamson, David, 33
Winton, Tim, 75, 134, 136, 137
Worrell, Frank, 117

Yes Minister, 159

www.ingramcontent.com/pod-product-compliance
Ingram Content Group UK Ltd.
Pitfield, Milton Keynes, MK11 3LW, UK
UKHW021324180426
11947UKWH00017B/1425